D1235056

DOVER · THRIFT · EDITIONS

Cornhuskers

CARL SANDBURG

DOVER PUBLICATIONS, INC.
Mineola, New York

DOVER THRIFT EDITIONS

GENERAL EDITOR: PAUL NEGRI
EDITOR OF THIS VOLUME: JOHN BERSETH

Bibliographical Note

This Dover edition, first published in 2000, contains the unabridged text of
Cornhuskers, first published by Henry Holt and Company, New York, in 1918. A
new Introductory Note and the alphabetical lists of titles and first lines have been
specially prepared for the present edition.
Acknowledgement is set forth that some things here were first printed in
Poetry: A Magazine of Verse, *The Chicago Daily News*, and the service of the
Newspaper Enterprise Association.—C. S.

Library of Congress Cataloging-in-Publication Data

Sandburg, Carl, 1878–1967.
    Cornhuskers / Carl Sandburg.
        p. cm.
    "A new introductory note and the alphabetical lists of titles and first lines
have been specially prepared for the present edition"—T.p. verso.
    Includes index.
    ISBN 0-486-41409-4 (pbk.)
    1. Middle West—Poetry. I. Title.

PS3537.A618 C7 2000
811'.52—dc20

00-031461

Manufactured in the United States of America
Dover Publications, Inc., 31 East 2nd Street, Mineola, N.Y. 11501

Note

CARL SANDBURG was born in Galesburg, Illinois, on January 6, 1878, the son of poor Swedish immigrants. Like many other boys in similar circumstances, he began working at an early age and held a variety of jobs—barbershop porter, milk wagon driver, brickyard worker, and itinerant wheat harvester. He enlisted in the 6th Illinois Infantry at the outbreak of the Spanish-American War and spent nine months in Puerto Rico. After discharge Sandburg attended Lombard College in Galesburg, where his first poetry was published in a pamphlet printed on a handpress. Politically, he was a populist, some said a radical. He worked as an organizer for the Wisconsin Social Democratic Party (1907–1908) and as secretary to Milwaukee's first Socialist mayor (1910–1912). In 1913 he moved to Chicago, where he became part of the "Chicago Renaissance" of arts and letters.

Sandburg's first success as a poet came with the publication of "Chicago" in Harriet Monroe's influential *Poetry* magazine in 1914; this poem and others were published in book form in 1916 as *Chicago Poems*. *Cornhuskers* was published two years later and received a special Pulitzer award in 1919. In addition to the title poem of this collection, of particular interest were "Caboose Thoughts," "Chicago Poet," "Haunts," and "Cool Tombs," a poem on death. Later books of poetry included *Smoke and Steel* (1920), *Slabs of the Sunburnt West* (1922), and *Good Morning, America* (1928). These collections reflected Sandburg's awareness of America as an increasingly urban, industrial nation. *The People, Yes* (1936), a sprawling collage of free verse and prose, constituted a kind of paean to Sandburg's beloved common folk, in all their American variety.

Sandburg also wrote and published prose in a variety of media. His exhaustive biography of Abraham Lincoln (2 vols., 1926; 4 vols.–1939) won a Pulitzer Prize. He was also awarded a Pulitzer for his *Complete Poems* (1950). He died July 22, 1967, on his farm in Flat Rock, North Carolina.

TO
JANET AND MARGARET

Contents

CORNHUSKERS

Prairie

I was born on the prairie and the milk of its wheat, the red of its
    clover, the eyes of its women, gave me a song and a slogan.

Here the water went down, the icebergs slid with gravel, the gaps
    and the valleys hissed, and the black loam came, and the yel-
    low sandy loam.
Here between the sheds of the Rocky Mountains and the
    Appalachians, here now a morning star fixes a fire sign over
    the timber claims and cow pastures, the corn belt, the cotton
    belt, the cattle ranches.
Here the gray geese go five hundred miles and back with a wind
    under their wings honking the cry for a new home.
Here I know I will hanker after nothing so much as one more sun-
    rise or a sky moon of fire doubled to a river moon of water.

The prairie sings to me in the forenoon and I know in the night I
    rest easy in the prairie arms, on the prairie heart.

* * *

    After the sunburn of the day
    handling a pitchfork at a hayrack,
    after the eggs and biscuit and coffee,
    the pearl-gray haystacks
    in the gloaming
    are cool prayers
    to the harvest hands.

In the city among the walls the overland passenger train is choked
    and the pistons hiss and the wheels curse.

1

On the prairie the overland flits on phantom wheels and the sky
and the soil between them muffle the pistons and cheer the
wheels.

● ● ●

I am here when the cities are gone.
I am here before the cities come.
I nourished the lonely men on horses.
I will keep the laughing men who ride iron.
I am dust of men.

The running water babbled to the deer, the cottontail, the go-
pher.
You came in wagons, making streets and schools,
Kin of the ax and rifle, kin of the plow and horse,
Singing *Yankee Doodle, Old Dan Tucker, Turkey in the Straw,*
You in the coonskin cap at a log house door hearing a lone wolf
howl,
You at a sod house door reading the blizzards and chinooks let
loose from Medicine Hat,
I am dust of your dust, as I am brother and mother
To the copper faces, the worker in flint and clay,
The singing women and their sons a thousand years ago
Marching single file the timber and the plain.

I hold the dust of these amid changing stars.
I last while old wars are fought, while peace broods mother-like,
While new wars arise and the fresh killings of young men.
I fed the boys who went to France in great dark days.
Appomattox is a beautiful word to me and so is Valley Forge and
the Marne and Verdun,
I who have seen the red births and the red deaths
Of sons and daughters, I take peace or war, I say nothing and
wait.

Have you seen a red sunset drip over one of my cornfields, the
shore of night stars, the wave lines of dawn up a wheat val-
ley?
Have you heard my threshing crews yelling in the chaff of a straw-
pile and the running wheat of the wagonboards, my corn-
huskers, my harvest hands hauling crops, singing dreams of
women, worlds, horizons?

● ● ●

Rivers cut a path on flat lands.
The mountains stand up.
The salt oceans press in
And push on the coast lines.
The sun, the wind, bring rain
And I know what the rainbow writes across
　　　　the east or west in a half-circle:
A love-letter pledge to come again.

●　　●　　●

Towns on the Soo Line,
Towns on the Big Muddy,
Laugh at each other for cubs
And tease as children.

Omaha and Kansas City, Minneapolis and St. Paul, sisters in a
　　house together, throwing slang, growing up.
Towns in the Ozarks, Dakota wheat towns, Wichita, Peoria,
　　Buffalo, sisters throwing slang, growing up.

●　　●　　●

Out of prairie-brown grass crossed with a streamer of wigwam
　　smoke—out of a smoke pillar, a blue promise—out of wild
　　ducks woven in greens and purples—
Here I saw a city rise and say to the peoples round world: Listen,
　　I am strong, I know what I want.
Out of log houses and stumps—canoes stripped from tree-sides—
　　flatboats coaxed with an ax from the timber claims—in the
　　years when the red and the white men met—the houses and
　　streets rose.

A thousand red men cried and went away to new places for corn
　　and women: a million white men came and put up sky-
　　scrapers, threw out rails and wires, feelers to the salt sea: now
　　the smokestacks bite the skyline with stub teeth.

In an early year the call of a wild duck woven in greens and pur-
　　ples: now the riveter's chatter, the police patrol, the song-
　　whistle of the steamboat.

To a man across a thousand years I offer a handshake.
I say to him: Brother, make the story short, for the stretch of a
　　thousand years is short.

• • •

What brothers these in the dark?
What eaves of skyscrapers against a smoke moon?
These chimneys shaking on the lumber shanties
When the coal boats plow by on the river—
The hunched shoulders of the grain elevators—
The flame sprockets of the sheet steel mills
And the men in the rolling mills with their shirts off
Playing their flesh arms against the twisting wrists of steel:
　　　　　　　　　what brothers these
　　　　　　　　　in the dark
　　　　　　　　　of a thousand years?

• • •

A headlight searches a snowstorm.
A funnel of white light shoots from over the pilot of the Pioneer
　　　Limited crossing Wisconsin.

In the morning hours, in the dawn,
The sun puts out the stars of the sky
And the headlight of the Limited train.

The fireman waves his hand to a country school teacher on a bob-
　　　sled.
A boy, yellow hair, red scarf and mittens, on the bobsled, in his
　　　lunch box a pork chop sandwich and a V of gooseberry pie.

The horses fathom a snow to their knees.
Snow hats are on the rolling prairie hills.
The Mississippi bluffs wear snow hats.

• • •

Keep your hogs on changing corn and mashes of grain,
　　　　O farmerman.
　　　　Cram their insides till they waddle on short legs
　　　　Under the drums of bellies, hams of fat.
　　　　Kill your hogs with a knife slit under the ear.
　　　　Hack them with cleavers.
　　　　Hang them with hooks in the hind legs.

• • •

A wagonload of radishes on a summer morning.
Sprinkles of dew on the crimson-purple balls.

The farmer on the seat dangles the reins on the rumps of dapple-
    gray horses.
The farmer's daughter with a basket of eggs dreams of a new hat
    to wear to the county fair.

• • •

On the left- and right-hand side of the road,
                Marching corn—
I saw it knee high weeks ago—now it is head high—tassels of red
    silk creep at the ends of the ears.

• • •

I am the prairie, mother of men, waiting.
They are mine, the threshing crews eating beefsteak, the farm-
    boys driving steers to the railroad cattle pens.
They are mine, the crowds of people at a Fourth of July basket
    picnic, listening to a lawyer read the Declaration of
    Independence, watching the pinwheels and Roman candles
    at night, the young men and women two by two hunting the
    bypaths and kissing bridges.
They are mine, the horses looking over a fence in the frost of late
    October saying good-morning to the horses hauling wagons
    of rutabaga to market.
They are mine, the old zigzag rail fences, the new barb wire.

• • •

The cornhuskers wear leather on their hands.
There is no let-up to the wind.
Blue bandannas are knotted at the ruddy chins.

Falltime and winter apples take on the smolder of the five-o'clock
    November sunset: falltime, leaves, bonfires, stubble, the old
    things go, and the earth is grizzled.
The land and the people hold memories, even among the
    anthills and the angleworms, among the toads and
    woodroaches—among gravestone writings rubbed out by the
    rain—they keep old things that never grow old.

The frost loosens corn husks.
The sun, the rain, the wind
        loosen corn husks.
The men and women are helpers.
They are all cornhuskers together.

I see them late in the western evening
       in a smoke-red dust.

• • •

The phantom of a yellow rooster flaunting a scarlet comb, on top
     of a dung pile crying hallelujah to the streaks of daylight,
The phantom of an old hunting dog nosing in the underbrush for
     muskrats, barking at a coon in a treetop at midnight, chew-
     ing a bone, chasing his tail round a corncrib,
The phantom of an old workhorse taking the steel point of a plow
     across a forty-acre field in spring, hitched to a harrow in
     summer, hitched to a wagon among cornshocks in fall,
These phantoms come into the talk and wonder of people on the
     front porch of a farmhouse late summer nights.
'The shapes that are gone are here," said an old man with a cob
     pipe in his teeth one night in Kansas with a hot wind on the
     alfalfa.

• • •

Look at six eggs
In a mockingbird's nest.

• • •

Listen to six mockingbirds
Flinging follies of O-be-joyful
Over the marshes and uplands.

Look at songs
Hidden in eggs.

• • •

When the morning sun is on the trumpet-vine blossoms, sing at
     the kitchen pans: Shout All Over God's Heaven.
When the rain slants on the potato hills and the sun plays a silver
     shaft on the last shower, sing to the bush at the backyard
     fence: Mighty Lak a Rose.
When the icy sleet pounds on the storm windows and the house
     lifts to a great breath, sing for the outside hills: The Ole
     Sheep Done Know the Road, the Young Lambs Must Find
     the Way.

• • •

Spring slips back with a girl face calling always: "Any new songs
for me? Any new songs?"

O prairie girl, be lonely, singing, dreaming, waiting—your lover
comes—your child comes—the years creep with toes of
April rain on new-turned sod.
O prairie girl, whoever leaves you only crimson poppies to talk
with, whoever puts a good-by kiss on your lips and never
comes back—
There is a song deep as the falltime red haws, long as the layer of
black loam we go to, the shine of the morning star over the
corn belt, the wave line of dawn up a wheat valley.

●　●　●

O prairie mother, I am one of your boys.
I have loved the prairie as a man with a heart shot full of pain over
love.
Here I know I will hanker after nothing so much as one more sun-
rise or a sky moon of fire doubled to a river moon of water.

●　●　●

I speak of new cities and new people.
I tell you the past is a bucket of ashes.
I tell you yesterday is a wind gone down,
a sun dropped in the west.
I tell you there is nothing in the world
only an ocean of to-morrows,
a sky of to-morrows.

I am a brother of the cornhuskers who say
at sundown:
To-morrow is a day.

River Roads

Let the crows go by hawking their caw and caw.
They have been swimming in midnights of coal mines some-
where.
Let 'em hawk their caw and caw.

Let the woodpecker drum and drum on a hickory stump.

He has been swimming in red and blue pools somewhere hundreds of years

And the blue has gone to his wings and the red has gone to his head.

Let his red head drum and drum.

Let the dark pools hold the birds in a looking-glass.

And if the pool wishes, let it shiver to the blur of many wings, old swimmers from old places.

Let the redwing streak a line of vermillion on the green wood lines.

And the mist along the river fix its purple in lines of a woman's shawl on lazy shoulders.

Prairie Waters by Night

Chatter of birds two by two raises a night song joining a litany of running water—sheer waters showing the russet of old stones remembering many rains.

And the long willows drowse on the shoulders of the running water, and sleep from much music; joined songs of day-end, feathery throats and stony waters, in a choir chanting new psalms.

It is too much for the long willows when low laughter of a red moon comes down; and the willows drowse and sleep on the shoulders of the running water.

Early Moon

The baby moon, a canoe, a silver papoose canoe, sails and sails in the Indian west.

A ring of silver foxes, a mist of silver foxes, sit and sit around the Indian moon.

One yellow star for a runner, and rows of blue stars for more runners, keep a line of watchers.

O foxes, baby moon, runners, you are the panel of memory, fire-
    white writing to-night of the Red Man's dreams.
Who squats, legs crossed and arms folded, matching its look
    against the moon-face, the star-faces, of the West?
Who are the Mississippi Valley ghosts, of copper foreheads, riding
    wiry ponies in the night?—no bridles, love-arms on the pony
    necks, riding in the night a long old trail?
Why do they always come back when the silver foxes sit around
    the early moon, a silver papoose, in the Indian west?

Laughing Corn

There was a high majestic fooling
Day before yesterday in the yellow corn.

And day after to-morrow in the yellow corn
There will be high majestic fooling.

The ears ripen in late summer
And come on with a conquering laughter,
Come on with a high and conquering laughter.

The long-tailed blackbirds are hoarse.
One of the smaller blackbirds chitters on a stalk
And a spot of red is on its shoulder
And I never heard its name in my life.

Some of the ears are bursting.
A white juice works inside.
Cornsilk creeps in the end and dangles in the wind.
Always—I never knew it any other way—
The wind and the corn talk things over together.
And the rain and the corn and the sun and the corn
Talk things over together.

Over the road is the farmhouse.
The siding is white and a green blind is slung loose.
It will not be fixed till the corn is husked.
The farmer and his wife talk things over together.

Autumn Movement

I cried over beautiful things knowing no beautiful thing lasts.

The field of cornflower yellow is a scarf at the neck of the copper sunburned woman, the mother of the year, the taker of seeds.

The northwest wind comes and the yellow is torn full of holes, new beautiful things come in the first spit of snow on the northwest wind, and the old things go, not one lasts.

Falltime

Gold of a ripe oat straw, gold of a southwest moon,
Canada thistle blue and flimmering larkspur blue,
Tomatoes shining in the October sun with red hearts,
Shining five and six in a row on a wooden fence,
Why do you keep wishes on your faces all day long,
Wishes like women with half-forgotten lovers going to new cities?
What is there for you in the birds, the birds, the birds, crying
    down on the north wind in September, acres of birds spot-
    ting the air going south?
Is there something finished? And some new beginning on the
    way?

Illinois Farmer

Bury this old Illinois farmer with respect.
He slept the Illinois nights of his life after days of work in Illinois
    cornfields.
Now he goes on a long sleep.
The wind he listened to in the cornsilk and the tassels, the wind
    that combed his red beard zero mornings when the snow lay
    white on the yellow ears in the bushel basket at the corncrib,
The same wind will now blow over the place here where his
    hands must dream of Illinois corn.

Hits and Runs

I remember the Chillicothe ball players grappling the Rock
    Island ball players in a sixteen-inning game ended by
    darkness.
And the shoulders of the Chillicothe players were a red smoke
    against the sundown and the shoulders of the Rock Island
    players were a yellow smoke against the sundown.
And the umpire's voice was hoarse calling balls and strikes and
    outs and the umpire's throat fought in the dust for a song.

Village in Late Summer

Lips half-willing in a doorway.
Lips half-singing at a window.
Eyes half-dreaming in the walls.
Feet half-dancing in a kitchen.
Even the clocks half-yawn the hours
And the farmers make half-answers.

Blizzard Notes

I don't blame the kettle drums—they are hungry.
And the snare drums—I know what they want—they are empty
    too.
And the harring booming bass drums—they are hungriest of all.

• • •

The howling spears of the Northwest die down.
The lullabies of the Southwest get a chance, a mother song.
A cradle moon rides out of a torn hole in the ragbag top of the sky.

Sunset From Omaha Hotel Window

Into the blue river hills
The red sun runners go
And the long sand changes
And to-day is a goner
And to-day is not worth haggling over.

> Here in Omaha
> The gloaming is bitter
> As in Chicago
> Or Kenosha.

The long sand changes.
To-day is a goner.
Time knocks in another brass nail.
Another yellow plunger shoots the dark.

> Constellations
> Wheeling over Omaha
> As in Chicago
> Or Kenosha.

The long sand is gone
          and all the talk is stars.
They circle in a dome over Nebraska.

Still Life

Cool your heels on the rail of an observation car.
Let the engineer open her up for ninety miles an hour.
Take in the prairie right and left, rolling land and new hay crops,
    swaths of new hay laid in the sun.
A gray village flecks by and the horses hitched in front of the post-
    office never blink an eye.
A barnyard and fifteen Holstein cows, dabs of white on a black
    wall map, never blink an eye.
A signalman in a tower, the outpost of Kansas City, keeps his
    place at a window with the serenity of a bronze statue on a
    dark night when lovers pass whispering.

Band Concert

Band concert public square Nebraska city. Flowing and circling
dresses, summer-white dresses. Faces, flesh tints flung like
sprays of cherry blossoms. And gigglers, God knows, gigglers,
rivaling the pony whinnies of the Livery Stable Blues.

Cowboy rags and nigger rags. And boys driving sorrel horses hurl
a cornfield laughter at the girls in dresses, summer-white
dresses. Amid the cornet staccato and the tuba oompa, gig-
glers, God knows, gigglers daffy with life's razzle dazzle.

Slow good-night melodies and Home Sweet Home. And the
snare drummer bookkeeper in a hardware store nods hello
to the daughter of a railroad conductor—a giggler, God
knows, a giggler—and the summer-white dresses filter fan-
wise out of the public square.

The crushed strawberries of ice cream soda places, the night wind
in cottonwoods and willows, the lattice shadows of doorsteps
and porches, these know more of the story.

Three Pieces on the Smoke of Autumn

Smoke of autumn is on it all.
The streamers loosen and travel.
The red west is stopped with a gray haze.
They fill the ash trees, they wrap the oaks,
They make a long-tailed rider
In the pocket of the first, the earliest evening star.

• • •

Three muskrats swim west on the Desplaines River.

There is a sheet of red ember glow on the river; it is dusk; and the
muskrats one by one go on patrol routes west.

Around each slippery padding rat, a fan of ripples; in the silence
of dusk a faint wash of ripples, the padding of the rats going
west, in a dark and shivering river gold.

(A newspaper in my pocket says the Germans pierce the Italian
   line; I have letters from poets and sculptors in Greenwich
   Village; I have letters from an ambulance man in France
   and an I. W. W. man in Vladivostok.)

I lean on an ash and watch the lights fall, the red ember glow, and
   three muskrats swim west in a fan of ripples on a sheet of
   river gold.

•   •   •

Better the blue silence and the gray west,
The autumn mist on the river,
And not any hate and not any love,
And not anything at all of the keen and the deep:
Only the peace of a dog head on a barn floor,
And the new corn shoveled in bushels
And the pumpkins brought from the corn rows,
Umber lights of the dark,
Umber lanterns of the loam dark.

Here a dog head dreams.
Not any hate, not any love.
Not anything but dreams.
Brother of dusk and umber.

Localities

Wagon Wheel Gap is a place I never saw
And Red Horse Gulch and the chutes of Cripple Creek.

Red-shirted miners picking in the sluices,
Gamblers with red neckties in the night streets,
The fly-by-night towns of Bull Frog and Skiddoo,
The night-cool limestone white of Death Valley,
The straight drop of eight hundred feet
From a shelf road in the Hasiampa Valley:
Men and places they are I never saw.

I have seen three White Horse taverns,
One in Illinois, one in Pennsylvania,
One in a timber-hid road of Wisconsin.

I bought cheese and crackers
Between sun showers in a place called White Pigeon
Nestling with a blacksmith shop, a post-office,
And a berry-crate factory, where four roads cross.

On the Pecatonica River near Freeport
I have seen boys run barefoot in the leaves
Throwing clubs at the walnut trees
In the yellow-and-gold of autumn,
And there was a brown mash dry on the inside of their hands.

On the Cedar Fork Creek of Knox County
I know how the fingers of late October
Loosen the hazel nuts.
I know the brown eyes of half-open hulls.
I know boys named Lindquist, Swanson, Hildebrand.
I remember their cries when the nuts were ripe.
And some are in machine shops; some are in the navy;
And some are not on payrolls anywhere.
Their mothers are through waiting for them to come home.

Caboose Thoughts

It's going to come out all right—do you know?
The sun, the birds, the grass—they know.
They get along—and we'll get along.

Some days will be rainy and you will sit waiting
And the letter you wait for won't come,
And I will sit watching the sky tear off gray and gray
And the letter I wait for won't come.

There will be ac-ci-dents.
I know ac-ci-dents are coming.
Smash-ups, signals wrong, washouts, trestles rotten,
Red and yellow ac-ci-dents.
But somehow and somewhere the end of the run
The train gets put together again
And the caboose and the green tail lights
Fade down the right of way like a new white hope.

I never heard a mockingbird in Kentucky
Spilling its heart in the morning.

I never saw the snow on Chimborazo.
It's a high white Mexican hat, I hear.

I never had supper with Abe Lincoln.
Nor a dish of soup with Jim Hill.

But I've been around.
I know some of the boys here who can go a little.
I know girls good for a burst of speed any time.

I heard Williams and Walker
Before Walker died in the bughouse.

I knew a mandolin player
Working in a barber shop in an Indiana town,
And he thought he had a million dollars.

I knew a hotel girl in Des Moines.
She had eyes; I saw her and said to myself
The sun rises and the sun sets in her eyes.
I was her steady and her heart went pit-a-pat.
We took away the money for a prize waltz at a Brotherhood
    dance.
She had eyes; she was safe as the bridge over the Mississippi at
    Burlington; I married her.

Last summer we took the cushions going west.
Pike's Peak is a big old stone, believe me.
It's fastened down; something you can count on.

It's going to come out all right—do you know?
The sun, the birds, the grass—they know.
They get along—and we'll get along.

Alix

The mare Alix breaks the world's trotting record one day. I see her
    heels flash down the dust of an Illinois race track on a sum-
    mer afternoon. I see the timekeepers put their heads to-
    gether over stopwatches, and call to the grand stand a split

second is clipped off the old world's record and a new
world's record fixed.

I see the mare Alix led away by men in undershirts and streaked
faces. Dripping Alix in foam of white on the harness and
shafts. And the men in undershirts kiss her ears and rub her
nose, and tie blankets on her, and take her away to have the
sweat sponged.

I see the grand stand jammed with prairie people yelling them-
selves hoarse. Almost the grand stand and the crowd of thou-
sands are one pair of legs and one voice standing up and
yelling hurrah.

I see the driver of Alix and the owner smothered in a fury of hand-
shakes, a mob of caresses. I see the wives of the driver and
owner smothered in a crush of white summer dresses and
parasols.

Hours later, at sundown, gray dew creeping on the sod and sheds,
I see Alix again:
> *Dark, shining-velvet Alix,*
> *Night-sky Alix in a gray blanket,*
> *Led back and forth by a nigger.*
> *Velvet and night-eyed Alix*
> *With slim legs of steel.*

And I want to rub my nose against the nose of the mare Alix.

Potato Blossom Songs and Jigs

> Rum tiddy um,
> tiddy um,
> tiddy um tum tum.

My knees are loose-like, my feet want to sling their selves.
I feel like tickling you under the chin—honey—and a-asking:
Why Does a Chicken Cross the Road?
When the hens are a-laying eggs, and the roosters pluck-pluck-
put-akut and you—honey—put new potatoes and gravy on
the table, and there ain't too much rain or too little:
> Say, why do I feel so gabby?
> Why do I want to holler all over the place?

• • •

Do you remember I held empty hands to you
    and I said all is yours
    the handfuls of nothing?

• • •

I ask you for white blossoms.
I bring a concertina after sunset under the apple trees.
I bring out "The Spanish Cavalier" and "In the Gloaming, O My
    Darling."

The orchard here is near and home-like.
The oats in the valley run a mile.
Between are the green and marching potato vines.
The lightning bugs go criss-cross carrying a zigzag of fire: the
    potato bugs are asleep under their stiff and yellow-striped
    wings: here romance stutters to the western stars, "Excuse
    . . . me . . ."

• • •

Old foundations of rotten wood.
An old barn done-for and out of the wormholes ten-legged
    roaches shook up and scared by sunlight.
So a pickax digs a long tooth with a short memory.
Fire can not eat this rubbish till it has lain in the sun.

• • •

The story lags.
The story has no connections.
The story is nothing but a lot of banjo plinka planka plunks.

The roan horse is young and will learn: the roan horse buckles
    into harness and feels the foam on the collar at the end of a
    haul: the roan horse points four legs to the sky and rolls in
    the red clover: the roan horse has a rusty jag of hair between
    the ears hanging to a white star between the eyes.

• • •

In Burlington long ago
And later again in Ashtabula
I said to myself:

I wonder how far Ophelia went with Hamlet.
What else was there Shakespeare never told?
There must have been something.
If I go bugs I want to do it like Ophelia.
There was class to the way she went out of her head.

• • •

Does a famous poet eat watermelon?
Excuse me, ask me something easy.
I have seen farmhands with their faces in fried catfish on a
    Monday morning.

And the Japanese, two-legged like us,
The Japanese bring slices of watermelon into pictures.
The black seeds make oval polka dots on the pink meat.

Why do I always think of niggers and buck-and-wing dancing
    whenever I see watermelon?

Summer mornings on the docks I walk among bushel peach bas-
    kets piled ten feet high.
Summer mornings I smell new wood and the river wind along
    with peaches.
I listen to the steamboat whistle hong-honging, hong-honging
    across the town.
And once I saw a teameo straddling a street with a hay-rack load
    of melons.

• • •

Niggers play banjos because they want to.
The explanation is easy.

It is the same as why people pay fifty cents for tickets to a police-
        men's masquerade ball or a grocers-and-butchers' picnic
        with a fat man's foot race.
It is the same as why boys buy a nickel's worth of peanuts and eat
        them and then buy another nickel's worth.
Newsboys shooting craps in a back alley have a fugitive under-
        standing of the scientific principle involved.
The jockey in a yellow satin shirt and scarlet boots, riding a sorrel
        pony at the county fair, has a grasp of the theory.

It is the same as why boys go running lickety-split
    away from a school-room geography lesson
    in April when the crawfishes come out
    and the young frogs are calling
    and the pussywillows and the cat-tails
    know something about geography themselves.

● ● ●

I ask you for white blossoms.
I offer you memories and people.
I offer you a fire zigzag over the green and marching vines.
I bring a concertina after supper under the home-like apple trees.
I make up songs about things to look at:
    potato blossoms in summer night mist filling the garden
        with white spots;
    a cavalryman's yellow silk handkerchief stuck in a flannel
        pocket over the left side of the shirt, over the ventricles
        of blood, over the pumps of the heart.

Bring a concertina after sunset under the apple trees.
Let romance stutter to the western stars, "Excuse . . . me . . ."

Loam

In the loam we sleep,
In the cool moist loam,
To the lull of years that pass
And the break of stars,

From the loam, then,
The soft warm loam,
  We rise:
To shape of rose leaf,
Of face and shoulder.

  We stand, then,
    To a whiff of life,
Lifted to the silver of the sun
Over and out of the loam
  A day.

Manitoba Childe Roland

Last night a January wind was ripping at the shingles over our house and whistling a wolf song under the eaves.

I sat in a leather rocker and read to a six-year-old girl the Browning poem, *Childe Roland to the Dark Tower Came.*

And her eyes had the haze of autumn hills and it was beautiful to her and she could not understand.

A man is crossing a big prairie, says the poem, and nothing happens—and he goes on and on—and it's all lonesome and empty and nobody home.

And he goes on and on—and nothing happens—and he comes on a horse's skull, dry bones of a dead horse—and you know more than ever it's all lonesome and empty and nobody home.

And the man raises a horn to his lips and blows—he fixes a proud neck and forehead toward the empty sky and the empty land—and blows one last wonder-cry.

And as the shuttling automatic memory of man clicks off its results willy-nilly and inevitable as the snick of a mouse-trap or the trajectory of a 42-centimeter projectile,

I flash to the form of a man to his hips in snow drifts of Manitoba and Minnesota—in the sled derby run from Winnipeg to Minneapolis.

He is beaten in the race the first day out of Winnipeg—the lead dog is eaten by four team mates—and the man goes on and on—running while the other racers ride—running while the other racers sleep—

Lost in a blizzard twenty-four hours, repeating a circle of travel hour after hour—fighting the dogs who dig holes in the snow and whimper for sleep—pushing on—running and walking five hundred miles to the end of the race—almost a winner—one toe frozen, feet blistered and frost-bitten.

And I know why a thousand young men of the Northwest meet him in the finishing miles and yell cheers—I know why judges of the race call him a winner and give him a special prize even though he is a loser.

I know he kept under his shirt and around his thudding heart amid the blizzards of five hundred miles that one last wonder-cry of Childe Roland—and I told the six-year-old girl all about it.

And while the January wind was ripping at the shingles and whistling a wolf song under the eaves, her eyes had the haze of autumn hills and it was beautiful to her and she could not understand.

Wilderness

There is a wolf in me . . . fangs pointed for tearing gashes . . . a red tongue for raw meat . . . and the hot lapping of blood— I keep this wolf because the wilderness gave it to me and the wilderness will not let it go.

There is a fox in me . . . a silver-gray fox . . . I sniff and guess . . . I pick things out of the wind and air . . . I nose in the dark night and take sleepers and eat them and hide the feathers . . . I circle and loop and double-cross.

There is a hog in me . . . a snout and a belly . . . a machinery for eating and grunting . . . a machinery for sleeping satisfied in the sun—I got this too from the wilderness and the wilderness will not let it go.

There is a fish in me . . . I know I came from salt-blue water-gates . . . I scurried with shoals of herring . . . I blew waterspouts with porpoises . . . before land was . . . before the water went down . . . before Noah . . . before the first chapter of Genesis.

There is a baboon in me . . . clambering-clawed . . . dog-faced . . . yawping a galoot's hunger . . . hairy under the armpits . . . here are the hawk-eyed hankering men . . . here are the blond and blue-eyed women . . . here they hide curled asleep waiting . . . ready to snarl and kill . . . ready to sing and give milk . . . waiting—I keep the baboon because the wilderness says so.

There is an eagle in me and a mockingbird . . . and the eagle flies among the Rocky Mountains of my dreams and fights among the Sierra crags of what I want . . . and the mockingbird warbles in the early forenoon before the dew is gone, warbles in the underbrush of my Chattanoogas of hope, gushes over the blue Ozark foothills of my wishes—And I got the eagle and the mockingbird from the wilderness.

O, I got a zoo, I got a menagerie, inside my ribs, under my bony head, under my red-valve heart—and I got something else: it is a man-child heart, a woman-child heart: it is a father and mother and lover: it came form God-Knows-Where: it is going to God-Knows-Where—For I am the keeper of the zoo: I say yes and no: I sing and kill and work: I am a pal of the world: I came from the wilderness.

PERSONS HALF KNOWN

Chicago Poet

I saluted a nobody.
I saw him in a looking-glass.
He smiled—so did I.
He crumpled the skin on his forehead,
    frowning—so did I.
Everything I did he did.
I said, "Hello, I know you."
And I was a liar to say so.

Ah, this looking-glass man!
Liar, fool, dreamer, play-actor,
Soldier, dusty drinker of dust—
Ah! he will go with me
Down the dark stairway
When nobody else is looking,
When everybody else is gone.

He locks his elbow in mine,
I lose all—but not him.

Fire-Logs

Nancy Hanks dreams by the fire;
Dreams, and the logs sputter,
And the yellow tongues climb.
Red lines lick their way in flickers.

Oh, sputter, logs.
    Oh, dream, Nancy.
Time now for a beautiful child.
Time now for a tall man to come.

Repetitions

They are crying salt tears
Over the beautiful beloved body
Of Inez Milholland,
Because they are glad she lived,
Because she loved open-armed,
Throwing love for a cheap thing
Belonging to everybody—
Cheap as sunlight,
And morning air.

Adelaide Crapsey

Among the bumble-bees in red-top hay, a freckled field of brown-
    eyed Susans dripping yellow leaves in July,
        I read your heart in a book.

And your mouth of blue pansy—I know somewhere I have seen
    it rain-shattered.

And I have seen a woman with her head flung between her naked
    knees, and her head held there listening to the sea, the great
    naked sea shouldering a load of salt.

And the blue pansy mouth sang to the sea:
    Mother of God, I'm so little a thing,
    Let me sing longer,
    Only a little longer.

And the sea shouldered its salt in long gray combers hauling new
    shapes on the beach sand.

Young Bullfrogs

Jimmy Wimbledon listened a first week in June.
Ditches along prairie roads of Northern Illinois
Filled the arch of night with young bullfrog songs.
Infinite mathematical metronomic croaks rose and spoke,
Rose and sang, rose in a choir of puzzles.
They made his head ache with riddles of music.
They rested his head with beaten cadence.
Jimmy Wimbledon listened.

Memoir of a Proud Boy

He lived on the wings of storm.
The ashes are in Chihuahua.

Out of Ludlow and coal towns in Colorado
Sprang a vengeance of Slav miners, Italians, Scots, Cornishmen,
    Yanks.
Killings ran under the spoken commands of this boy
With eighty men and rifles on a hogback mountain.

They killed swearing to remember
The shot and charred wives and children
In the burnt camp of Ludlow,
And Louis Tikas, the laughing Greek,
Plugged with a bullet, clubbed with a gun butt.

As a home war
It held the nation a week
And one or two million men stood together
And swore by the retribution of steel.

It was all accidental.
He lived flecking lint off coat lapels
Of men he talked with.
He kissed the miners' babies
And wrote a Denver paper
Of picket silhouettes on a mountain line.

He had no mother but Mother Jones
Crying from a jail window of Trinidad:

"All I want is room enough to stand
And shake my fist at the enemies of the human race."

Named by a grand jury as a murderer
He went to Chihuahua, forgot his old Scotch name,
Smoked cheroots with Pancho Villa
And wrote letters of Villa as a rock of the people.

How can I tell how Don Magregor went?

Three riders emptied lead into him.
He lay on the main street of an inland town.
A boy sat near all day throwing stones
To keep pigs away.

The Villa men buried him in a pit
With twenty Carranzistas.

There is drama in that point . . .
. . . the boy and the pigs.
Griffith would make a movie of it to fetch sobs.
Victor Herbert would have the drums whirr
In a weave with a high fiddle-string's single clamor.

"And the muchacho sat there all day throwing stones
To keep the pigs away," wrote Gibbons to the *Tribune*.

Somewhere in Chihuahua or Colorado
Is a leather bag of poems and short stories.

Bilbea
(From tablet writing, Babylonian excavations of 4th millennium B.C.)

Bilbea, I was in Babylon on Saturday night.
I saw nothing of you anywhere.
I was at the old place and the other girls were there, but no
    Bilbea.

Have you gone to another house? or city?
Why don't you write?
I was sorry. I walked home half-sick.

Tell me how it goes.
Send me some kind of a letter.
And take care of yourself.

Southern Pacific

Huntington sleeps in a house six feet long.
Huntington dreams of railroads he built and owned.
Huntington dreams of ten thousand men saying: Yes, sir.

Blithery sleeps in a house six feet long.
Blithery dreams of rails and ties he laid.
Blithery dreams of saying to Huntington: Yes, sir.

Huntington,
Blithery, sleep in houses six feet long.

Washerwoman

The washerwoman is a member of the Salvation Army.
And over the tub of suds rubbing underwear clean
She sings that Jesus will wash her sins away
And the red wrongs she has done God and man
Shall be white as driven snow.
Rubbing underwear she sings of the Last Great Washday.

Portrait of a Motor Car

It's a lean car . . . a long-legged dog of a car . . . a gray-ghost eagle
    car.
The feet of it eat the dirt of a road . . . the wings of it eat the hills.
Danny the driver dreams of it when he sees women in red skirts
    and red sox in his sleep.
It is in Danny's life and runs in the blood of him . . . a lean gray-
    ghost car.

Girl in a Cage

Here in a cage the dollars come down.
To the click of a tube the dollars tumble.
And out of a mouth the dollars run.

    I finger the dollars,
    Paper and silver,
    Thousands a day.

Some days it's fun
      to finger the dollars.
Some days . . .
      the dollars keep on
      in a sob or a whisper:
    A flame of rose in the hair,
    A flame of silk at the throat.

Buffalo Bill

Boy heart of Johnny Jones—aching to-day?
Aching, and Buffalo Bill in town?
Buffalo Bill and ponies, cowboys, Indians?

Some of us know
All about it, Johnny Jones.

Buffalo Bill is a slanting look of the eyes,
    A slanting look under a hat on a horse.
He sits on a horse and a passing look is fixed
    On Johnny Jones, you and me, barelegged,
A slanting, passing, careless look under a hat on a horse.

Go clickety-clack, O pony hoofs along the street.
Come on and slant your eyes again, O Buffalo Bill.
Give us again the ache of our boy hearts.
Fill us again with the red love of prairies, dark nights, lonely
      wagons, and the crack-crack of rifles sputtering flashes into
      an ambush.

Sixteen Months

On the lips of the child Janet float changing dreams.
It is a thin spiral of blue smoke,
A morning campfire at a mountain lake.

On the lips of the child Janet,
Wisps of haze on ten miles of corn,
Young light blue calls to young light gold of morning.

Child Margaret

The child Margaret begins to write numbers on a Saturday morn-
ing, the first numbers formed under her wishing child fin-
gers.
All the numbers come well-born, shaped in figures assertive for a
frieze in a child's room.
Both 1 and 7 are straightforward, military, filled with lunge and
attack, erect in shoulder-straps.
The 6 and 9 salute as dancing sisters, elder and younger, and 2 is
a trapeze actor swinging to handclaps.
All the numbers are well-born, only 3 has a hump on its back and
8 is knock-kneed.
The child Margaret kisses all once and gives two kisses to 3 and
8.
(Each number is a bran-new rag doll . . . O in the wishing fingers
. . . millions of rag dolls, millions and millions of new rag
dolls!!)

Singing Nigger

Your bony head, Jazbo, O dock walloper,
Those grappling hooks, those wheelbarrow handlers,
The dome and the wings of you, nigger,
The red roof and the door of you,
I know where your songs came from.
I know why God listens to your, "Walk All Over God's Heaven."

I heard you shooting craps, "My baby's going to have a new dress."

I heard you in the cinders, "I'm going to live anyhow until I die."

I saw five of you with a can of beer on a summer night and I listened to the five of you harmonizing six ways to sing, "Way Down Yonder in the Cornfield."

I went away asking where I come from.

LEATHER LEGGINGS

Leather Leggings

They have taken the ball of earth
    and made it a little thing.

They were held to the land and horses;
    they were held to the little seas.
They have changed and shaped and welded;
    they have broken the old tools and made
    new ones; they are ranging the white
    scarves of cloudland; they are bumping
    the sunken bells of the Carthaginians
    and Phœnicians:
        they are handling
        the strongest sea
        as a thing to be handled.

The earth was a call that mocked;
    it is belted with wires and meshed with
    steel; from Pittsburg to Vladivostok is
    an iron ride on a moving house; from
    Jerusalem to Tokyo is a reckoned span;
    and they talk at night in the storm and
    salt, the wind and the war.

They have counted the miles to the Sun
    and Canopus; they have weighed a small
    blue star that comes in the southeast
    corner of the sky on a foretold errand.

We shall search the sea again.
We shall search the stars again.

There are no bars across the way.
There is no end to the plan and the clue,
    the hunt and the thirst.
The motors are drumming, the leather leggings
    and the leather coats wait:
        Under the sea
        and out to the stars
        we go.

Prayers of Steel

Lay me on an anvil, O God.
Beat me and hammer me into a crowbar.
Let me pry loose old walls.
Let me lift and loosen old foundations.

Lay me on an anvil, O God.
Beat me and hammer me into a steel spike.
Drive me into the girders that hold a skyscraper together.
Take red-hot rivets and fasten me into the central girders.
Let me be the great nail holding a skyscraper through blue nights
    into white stars.

Always the Mob

Jesus emptied the devils of one man into forty hogs and the hogs
    took the edge of a high rock and dropped off and down into
    the sea: a mob.

The sheep on the hills of Australia, blundering four-footed in the
    sunset mist to the dark, they go one way, they hunt one
    sleep, they find one pocket of grass for all.

Karnak? Pyramids? Sphinx paws tall as a coolie? Tombs kept for
    kings and sacred cows? A mob.

Young roast pigs and naked dancing girls of Belshazzar, the room
    where a thousand sat guzzling when a hand wrote: Mene,
    mene, tekel, upharsin? A mob.

The honeycomb of green that won the sun as the Hanging
Gardens of Nineveh, flew to its shape at the hands of a mob
that followed the fingers of Nebuchadnezzar: a mob of one
hand and one plan.

Stones of a circle of hills at Athens, staircases of a mountain in
Peru, scattered clans of marble dragons in China: each a
mob on the rim of a sunrise: hammers and wagons have
them now.

Locks and gates of Panama? The Union Pacific crossing deserts
and tunneling mountains? The Woolworth on land and the
Titanic at sea? Lighthouses blinking a coast line from
Labrador to Key West? Pigiron bars piled on a barge
whistling in a fog off Sheboygan? A mob: hammers and wag-
ons have them to-morrow.

The mob? A typhoon tearing loose an island from thousand-year
moorings and bastions, shooting a volcanic ash with a fire
tongue that licks up cities and peoples. Layers of worms eat-
ing rocks and forming loam and valley floors for potatoes,
wheat, watermelons.

The mob? A jag of lightning, a geyser, a gravel mass loosening . . .

The mob . . . kills or builds . . . the mob is Attila or Ghengis Khan,
the mob is Napoleon, Lincoln.

I am born in the mob—I die in the mob—the same goes for
you—I don't care who you are.

I cross the sheets of fire in No Man's land for you, my brother—
I slip a steel tooth into your throat, you my brother—I die
for you and I kill you—It is a twisted and gnarled thing,
a crimson wool:

> One more arch of stars,
> In the night of our mist,
> In the night of our tears.

Jabberers

I rise out of my depths with my language.
You rise out of your depths with your language.

Two tongues from the depths,
Alike only as a yellow cat and a green parrot are alike,
Fling their staccato tantalizations
Into a wildcat jabber
Over a gossamer web of unanswerables.

The second and the third silence,
Even the hundredth silence,
Is better than no silence at all
(Maybe this is a jabber too—are we at it again, you and I?)

I rise out of my depths with my language.
You rise out of your depths with your language.

One thing there is much of; the name men call it by is time; into
this gulf our syllabic pronunciamentos empty by the way
rockets of fire curve and are gone on the night sky; into this
gulf the jabberings go as the shower at a scissors grinder's
wheel. . . .

Cartoon

I am making a Cartoon of a Woman. She is the People. She is the
Great Dirty Mother.
And Many Children hang on her Apron, crawl at her Feet, snug-
gle at her Breasts.

Interior

In the cool of the night time
The clocks pick off the points
And the mainsprings loosen.
They will need winding.
One of these days . . .
                they will need winding.

Rabelais in red boards,
Walt Whitman in green,
Hugo in ten-cent paper covers,
Here they stand on shelves

In the cool of the night time
And there is nothing . . .
To be said against them . . .
Or for them . . .
In the cool of the night time
And the clocks.

A man in pigeon-gray pyjamas.
The open window begins at his feet
And goes taller than his head.
Eight feet high is the pattern.

Moon and mist make an oblong layout.
Silver at the man's bare feet.
He swings one foot in a moon silver.
And it costs nothing.

One more day of bread and work.
One more day . . . so much rags . . .
The man barefoot in moon silver
Mutters "You" and "You"
To things hidden
In the cool of the night time,
In Rabelais, Whitman, Hugo,
In an oblong of moon mist.

Out from the window . . . prairielands.
Moon mist whitens a golf ground.
Whiter yet is a limestone quarry.
The crickets keep on chirring.

Switch engines of the Great Western
Sidetrack box cars, make up trains
For Weehawken, Oskaloosa, Saskatchewan;
The cattle, the coal, the corn, must go
In the night . . . on the prairielands.

Chuff-chuff go the pulses.
They beat in the cool of the night time.
Chuff-chuff and chuff-chuff . . .
These heartbeats travel the night a mile
And touch the moon silver at the window
And the bones of the man.
It costs nothing.

Rabelais in red boards,
Whitman in green,
Hugo in ten-cent paper covers,
Here they stand on shelves
In the cool of the night time
And the clocks.

Street Window

The pawn-shop man knows hunger,
And how far hunger has eaten the heart
Of one who comes with an old keepsake.
Here are wedding rings and baby bracelets,
Scarf pins and shoe buckles, jeweled garters,
Old-fashioned knives with inlaid handles,
Watches of old gold and silver,
Old coins worn with finger-marks.
They tell stories.

Palladiums

In the newspaper office—who are the spooks?
Who wears the mythic coat invisible?

Who pussyfoots from desk to desk
            with a speaking forefinger?
Who gumshoes amid the copy paper
            with a whispering thumb?

Speak softly—the sacred cows may hear.
Speak easy—the sacred cows must be fed.

Clocks

Here is a face that says half-past seven the same way whether a
    murder or a wedding goes on, whether a funeral or a picnic
    crowd passes.

A tall one I know at the end of a hallway broods in shadows and is watching booze eat out the insides of the man of the house; it has seen five hopes go in five years: one woman, one child, and three dreams.

A little one carried in a leather box by an actress rides with her to hotels and is under her pillow in a sleeping-car between one-night stands.

One hoists a phiz over a railroad station; it points numbers to people a quarter-mile away who believe it when other clocks fail.

And of course . . . there are wrist watches over the pulses of air-men eager to go to France . . .

Legends

CLOWNS DYING

Five circus clowns dying this year, morning newspapers told their lives, how each one horizontal in a last gesture of hands arranged by an undertaker, shook thousands into convulsions of laughter from behind rouge-red lips and powder-white face.

STEAMBOAT BILL

When the boilers of the *Robert E. Lee* exploded, a steamboat winner of many races on the Mississippi went to the bottom of the river and never again saw the wharves of Natchez and New Orleans.

And a legend lives on that two gamblers were blown toward the sky and during their journey laid bets on which of the two would go higher and which would be first to set foot on the turf of the earth again.

FOOT AND MOUTH PLAGUE

When the mysterious foot and mouth epidemic ravaged the cattle of Illinois, Mrs. Hector Smith wept bitterly over the government killing forty of her soft-eyed Jersey cows; through the newspapers she wept over her loss for millions of readers in the Great Northwest.

SEVENS

The lady who has had seven lawful husbands has written seven
years for a famous newspaper telling how to find love and
keep it: seven thousand hungry girls in the Mississippi Valley
have read the instructions seven years and found neither il-
licit lovers nor lawful husbands.

PROFITEER

I who saw ten strong young men die anonymously, I who saw ten
old mothers hand over their sons to the nation anonymously,
I who saw ten thousand touch the sunlit silver finalities of
undistinguished human glory—why do I sneeze sardonically
at a bronze drinking fountain named after one who partici-
pated in the war vicariously and bought ten farms?

Psalm of Those Who Go Forth Before Daylight

The policeman buys shoes slow and careful; the teamster buys
gloves slow and careful; they take care of their feet and
hands; they live on their feet and hands.

The milkman never argues; he works alone and no one speaks
to him; the city is asleep when he is on the job; he puts a
bottle on six hundred porches and calls it a day's work; he
climbs two hundred wooden stairways; two horses are com-
pany for him; he never argues.

The rolling-mill men and the sheet-steel men are brothers of cin-
ders; they empty cinders out of their shoes after the day's
work; they ask their wives to fix burnt holes in the knees of
their trousers; their necks and ears are covered with a smut;
they scour their necks and ears; they are brothers of cinders.

Horses and Men in Rain

Let us sit by a hissing steam radiator a winter's day, gray wind pat-
tering frozen raindrops on the window,

And let us talk about milk wagon drivers and grocery delivery boys.

Let us keep our feet in wool slippers and mix hot punches—and talk about mail carriers and messenger boys slipping along the icy sidewalks.

Let us write of olden, golden days and hunters of the Holy Grail and men called "knights" riding horses in the rain, in the cold frozen rain for ladies they loved.

A roustabout hunched on a coal wagon goes by, icicles drip on his hat rim, sheets of ice wrapping the hunks of coal, the caravanserai a gray blur in slant of rain.

Let us nudge the steam radiator with our wool slippers and write poems of Launcelot, the hero, and Roland, the hero, and all the olden golden men who rode horses in the rain.

Questionnaire

Have I told any man to be a liar for my sake?

Have I sold ice to the poor in summer and coal to the poor in winter for the sake of daughters who nursed brindle bull terriers and led with a leash their dogs clothed in plaid wool jackets?

Have I given any man an earful too much of my talk—or asked any man to take a snootful of booze on my account?

Have I put wool in my own ears when men tried to tell me what was good for me? Have I been a bum listener?

Have I taken dollars from the living and the unborn while I made speeches on the retributions that shadow the heels of the dishonest?

Have I done any good under cover? Or have I always put it in the show windows and the newspapers?

Near Keokuk

Thirty-two Greeks are dipping their feet in a creek.
Sloshing their bare feet in a cool flow of clear water.

All one midsummer day ten hours the Greeks
        stand in leather shoes shoveling gravel.
Now they hold their toes and ankles
        to the drift of running water.
Then they go to the bunk cars
        and eat mulligan and prune sauce,
Smoke one or two pipefuls, look at the stars,
        tell smutty stories
About men and women they have known,
        countries they have seen,
Railroads they have built—
        and then the deep sleep of children.

Slants at Buffalo, New York

A forefinger of stone, dreamed by a sculptor, points to the sky.
It says: This way! this way!

Four lions snore in stone at the corner of the shaft.
They too are the dream of a sculptor.
They too say: This way! this way!

The street cars swing at a curve.
The middle-class passengers witness low life.
The car windows frame low life all day in pictures.

Two Italian cellar delicatessens
                sell red and green peppers.
The Florida bananas furnish a burst of yellow.
The lettuce and the cabbage give a green.

Boys play marbles in the cinders.
The boys' hands need washing.
The boys are glad; they fight among each other.

A plank bridge leaps the Lehigh Valley railroad.
Then acres of steel rails, freight cars, smoke,
And then . . . the blue lake shore
. . . Erie with Norse blue eyes . . . and the white sun.

Flat Lands

Flat lands on the end of town where real estate men are crying
    new subdivisions,
The sunsets pour blood and fire over you hundreds and hundreds
    of nights, flat lands—blood and fire of sunsets thousands of
    years have been pouring over you.
And the stars follow the sunsets. One gold star. A shower of blue
    stars. Blurs of white and gray stars. Vast marching proces-
    sions of stars arching over you flat lands where frogs sob this
    April night.
"Lots for Sale—Easy Terms" run letters painted on a board—and
    the stars wheel onward, the frogs sob this April night.

Lawyer

When the jury files in to deliver a verdict after weeks of direct and
    cross examinations, hot clashes of lawyers and cool decisions
    of the judge,
There are points of high silence—twiddling of thumbs is at an
    end—bailiffs near cuspidors take fresh chews of tobacco and
    wait—and the clock has a chance for its ticking to be heard.
A lawyer for the defense clears his throat and holds himself ready
    if the word is "Guilty" to enter motion for a new trial, speak-
    ing in a soft voice, speaking in a voice slightly colored with
    bitter wrongs mingled with monumental patience, speaking
    with mythic Atlas shoulders of many preposterous, unjust
    circumstances.

Three Balls

Jabowsky's place is on a side street and only the rain washes the
    dusty three balls.
When I passed the window a month ago, there rested in proud
    isolation:
A family bible with hasps of brass twisted off, a wooden clock with
    pendulum gone,

And a porcelain crucifix with the glaze nicked where the left elbow of Jesus is represented.

I passed to-day and they were all there, resting in proud isolation, the clock and the crucifix saying no more and no less than before, and a yellow cat sleeping in a patch of sun alongside the family bible with the hasps off.

Only the rain washes the dusty three balls in front of Jabowsky's place on a side street.

Chicks

The chick in the egg picks at the shell, cracks open one oval world, and enters another oval world.

"Cheep . . . cheep . . . cheep" is the salutation of the newcomer, the emigrant, the casual at the gates of the new world.

"Cheep . . . cheep" . . . from oval to oval, sunset to sunset, star to star.

It is at the door of this house, this teeny weeny eggshell exit, it is here men say a riddle and jeer each other: who are you? where do you go from here?

(In the academies many books, at the circus many sacks of peanuts, at the club rooms many cigar butts.)

"Cheep . . . cheep" . . . from oval to oval, sunset to sunset, star to star.

Humdrum

If I had a million lives to live
        and a million deaths to die
        in a million humdrum worlds,
I'd like to change my name
        and have a new house number to go by
        each and every time I died
        and started life all over again.

I wouldn't want the same name every time
    and the same old house number always,
    dying a million deaths,
    dying one by one a million times:
    —would you?
              or you?
                  or you?

Joliet

On the one hand the steel works.
On the other hand the penitentiary.
Santa Fé trains and Alton trains
Between smokestacks on the west
And gray walls on the east.
And Lockport down the river.

Part of the valley is God's.
And part is man's.
The river course laid out
A thousand years ago.
The canals ten years back.

The sun on two canals and one river
Makes three stripes of silver
Or copper and gold
Or shattered sunflower leaves.
    Talons of an iceberg
    Scraped out this valley.
    Claws of an avalanche loosed here.

Knucks

In Abraham Lincoln's city,
Where they remember his lawyer's shingle,
The place where they brought him
Wrapped in battle flags,
Wrapped in the smoke of memories

From Tallahassee to the Yukon,
The place now where the shaft of his tomb
Points white against the blue prairie dome,
In Abraham Lincoln's city . . . I saw knucks
In the window of Mister Fischman's second-hand store
On Second Street.

I went in and asked, "How much?"
"Thirty cents apiece," answered Mister Fischman.
And taking a box of new ones off a shelf
He filled anew the box in the showcase
And said incidentally, most casually
And incidentally:
"I sell a carload a month of these."

I slipped my fingers into a set of knucks,
Cast-iron knucks molded in a foundry pattern,
And there came to me a set of thoughts like these:
Mister Fischman is for Abe and the "malice to none" stuff,
And the street car strikers and the strike-breakers,
And the sluggers, gunmen, detectives, policemen,
Judges, utility heads, newspapers, priests, lawyers,
They are all for Abe and the "malice to none" stuff.

I started for the door.
"Maybe you want a lighter pair,"
Came Mister Fischman's voice.
I opened the door . . . and the voice again:
"You are a funny customer."

Wrapped in battle flags,
Wrapped in the smoke of memories,
This is the place they brought him,
This is Abraham Lincoln's home town.

Testament

I give the undertakers permission to haul my body
to the graveyard and to lay away all, the head, the
feet, the hands, all: I know there is something left
over they can not put away.

Let the nanny goats and the billy goats of the shanty
people eat the clover over my grave   and if any yellow
hair or any blue smoke of flowers is good enough to grow
over me   let the dirty-fisted children of the shanty
people pick these flowers.

I have had my chance to live with the people who have
too much and the people who have too little and I chose
one of the two and I have told no man why.

HAUNTS

Valley Song

Your eyes and the valley are memories.
Your eyes fire and the valley a bowl.
It was here a moonrise crept over the timberline.
It was here we turned the coffee cups upside down.
And your eyes and the moon swept the valley.

I will see you again to-morrow.
I will see you again in a million years.
I will never know your dark eyes again.
These are three ghosts I keep.
These are three sumach-red dogs I run with.

All of it wraps and knots to a riddle:
I have the moon, the timberline, and you.
All three are gone—and I keep all three.

In Tall Grass

Bees and a honeycomb in the dried head of a horse in a pasture
    corner—a skull in the tall grass and a buzz and a buzz of the
    yellow honey-hunters.

And I ask no better a winding sheet
               (over the earth and under the sun.)

Let the bees go honey-hunting with yellow blur of wings in the
    dome of my head, in the rumbling, singing arch of my skull.

Let there be wings and yellow dust and the drone of dreams of
     honey—who loses and remembers?—who keeps and for-
     gets?

In a blue sheen of moon over the bones and under the hanging
     honeycomb the bees come home and the bees sleep.

Upstairs

I too have a garret of old playthings.
I have tin soldiers with broken arms upstairs.
I have a wagon and the wheels gone upstairs.
I have guns and a drum, a jumping-jack and a magic lantern.
And dust is on them and I never look at them upstairs.
I too have a garret of old playthings.

Monosyllabic

Let me be monosyllabic to-day, O Lord.
Yesterday I loosed a snarl of words on a fool,
          on a child.
To-day, let me be monosyllabic . . . a crony of old men
          who wash sunlight in their fingers and
          enjoy slow-pacing clocks.

Films

I have kept all, not one is thrown away, not one given to the rag-
     man, not one thrust in a corner with a "P-f-f."
The red ones and the blue, the long ones in stripes, and each of
     the little black and white checkered ones.
Keep them: I tell my heart: keep them another year, another ten
     years: they will be wanted again.
They came once, they came easy, they came like a first white
     flurry of snow in late October,

Like any sudden, presumptuous, beautiful thing, and they were
  cheap at the price, cheap like snow.
Here a red one and there a long one in yellow stripes,
O there shall be no ragman have these yet a year, yet ten years.

Kreisler

Sell me a violin, mister, of old mysterious wood.
Sell me a fiddle that has kissed dark nights on the forehead where
  men kiss sisters they love.
Sell me dried wood that has ached with passion clutching the
  knees and arms of a storm.
Sell me horsehair and rosin that has sucked at the breasts of the
  morning sun for milk.
Sell me something crushed in the heartsblood of pain readier
  than ever for one more song.

The Sea Hold

The sea is large.
The sea hold on a leg of land in the Chesapeake hugs an early
  sunset and a last morning star over the oyster beds and the
  late clam boats of lonely men.
Five white houses on a half-mile strip of land . . . five white dice
  rolled from a tube.

Not so long ago . . . the sea was large . . .
And to-day the sea has lost nothing . . . it keeps all.

I am a loon about the sea.
I make so many sea songs, I cry so many sea cries, I forget so many
  sea songs and sea cries.

I am a loon about the sea.
So are five men I had a fish fry with once in a tar-paper shack
  trembling in a sand storm.
The sea knows more about them than they know themselves.
They know only how the sea hugs and will not let go.

The sea is large.
The sea must know more than any of us.

Goldwing Moth

A goldwing moth is between the scissors and the ink bottle on the
 desk.
Last night it flew hundreds of circles around a glass bulb and a
 flame wire.
The wings are a soft gold; it is the gold of illuminated initials in
 manuscripts of the medieval monks.

Loin Cloth

Body of Jesus taken down from the cross
Carved in ivory by a lover of Christ,
It is a child's handful you are here,
The breadth of a man's finger,
And this ivory loin cloth
Speaks an interspersal in the day's work,
The carver's prayer and whim
And Christ-love.

Hemlock and Cedar

Thin sheets of blue smoke among white slabs . . . near the shin-
 gle mill . . . winter morning.
Falling of a dry leaf might be heard . . . circular steel tears through
 a log.
Slope of woodland . . . brown . . . soft . . . tinge of blue such as
 pansy eyes.
Farther, field fires . . . funnel of yellow smoke . . . spellings of
 other yellow in corn stubble.
Bobsled on a down-hill road . . . February snow mud . . . horses
 steaming . . . Oscar the driver sings ragtime under a spot of
 red seen a mile . . . the red wool yarn of Oscar's stocking cap
 is seen from the shingle mill to the ridge of hemlock and
 cedar.

Summer Shirt Sale

The summer shirt sale of a downtown haberdasher is glorified in a show-window slang: everybody understands the language: red dots, yellow circles, blue anchors, and dove-brown hooks, these perform explosions in color: stripes and checks fight for the possession of front lines and salients: detectives, newsies, teameoes, niggers, all stop, look, and listen: the shirt sale and the show window kick at the street with a noise joyous as a clog dancer: the ensemble is a challenge to the ghost who walks on paydays.

Medallion

The brass medallion profile of your face I keep always.
It is not jingling with loose change in my pockets.
It is not stuck up in a show place on the office wall.
I carry it in a special secret pocket in the day
And it is under my pillow at night.
The brass came from a long ways off: it was up against hell and
      high water, fire and flood, before the face was put on it.
It is the side of a head; a woman wishes; a woman waits; a woman
      swears behind silent lips that the sea will bring home what is
      gone.

Bricklayer Love

I thought of killing myself because I am only a bricklayer and you
      a woman who loves the man who runs a drug store.

I don't care like I used to; I lay bricks straighter than I used to and
      I sing slower handling the trowel afternoons.

When the sun is in my eyes and the ladders are shaky and the
      mortar boards go wrong, I think of you.

Ashurnatsirpal III

(From Babylonian tablet, 4,000 years Before Christ)

Three walls around the town of Tela when I came.
They expected everything of those walls;
Nobody in the town came out to kiss my feet.

I knocked the walls down, killed three thousand soldiers,
Took away cattle and sheep, took all the loot in sight,
And burned special captives.

Some of the soldiers—I cut off hands and feet.
Others—I cut off ears and fingers.
Some—I put out the eyes.
I made a pyramid of heads.
I strung heads on trees circling the town.

When I got through with it
There wasn't much left of the town of Tela.

Mammy Hums

This is the song I rested with:
The right shoulder of a strong man I leaned on.
The face of the rain that drizzled on the short neck of a canal
    boat.
The eyes of a child who slept while death went over and under.
The petals of peony pink that fluttered in a shot of wind come
    and gone.

This is the song I rested with:
Head, heels, and fingers rocked to the nigger mammy humming
    of it, to the mile-off steamboat landing whistle of it.

The murmurs run with bees' wings
                    in a late summer sun.
They go and come with white surf
                    slamming on a beach all day.

    Get this.
And then you may sleep with a late afternoon slumber sun.

Then you may slip your head in an elbow knowing nothing—
 only sleep.
If so you sleep in the house of our song,
If so you sleep under the apple trees of our song,
Then the face of sleep must be the one face you were looking for.

Bringers

Cover me over
In dusk and dust and dreams.

Cover me over
And leave me alone.

Cover me over,
You tireless, great.

Hear me and cover me,
Bringers of dusk and dust and dreams.

Crimson Rambler

Now that a crimson rambler
 begins to crawl over the house
 of our two lives—

Now that a red curve
 winds across the shingles—

Now that hands
 washed in early sunrises
 climb and spill scarlet
 on a white lattice weave—

Now that a loop of blood
 is written on our roof
 and reaching around a chimney—

How are the two lives of this house
 to keep strong hands and strong hearts?

Haunts

There are places I go when I am strong.
One is a marsh pool where I used to go
        with a long-ear hound-dog.
One is a wild crabapple tree; I was there
        a moonlight night with a girl.
The dog is gone; the girl is gone; I go to these
        places when there is no other place to go.

Have Me

Have me in the blue and the sun.
Have me on the open sea and the mountains.

When I go into the grass of the sea floor, I will go alone.
This is where I came from—the chlorine and the salt are blood
    and bones.
It is here the nostrils rush the air to the lungs. It is here oxygen
    clamors to be let in.
And here in the root grass of the sea floor I will go alone.

Love goes far. Here love ends.
Have me in the blue and the sun.

Fire Dreams

(Written to be read aloud, if so be, Thanksgiving Day)

I remember here by the fire,
In the flickering reds and saffrons,
They came in a ramshackle tub,
Pilgrims in tall hats,
Pilgrims of iron jaws,
Drifting by weeks on beaten seas,
And the random chapters say
They were glad and sang to God.

And so
Since the iron-jawed men sat down

And said, "Thanks, O God,"
For life and soup and a little less
Than a hobo handout to-day,
Since gray winds blew gray patterns of sleet on Plymouth Rock,
Since the iron-jawed men sang "Thanks, O God,"
You and I, O Child of the West,
Remember more than ever
November and the hunter's moon,
November and the yellow-spotted hills.

And so
In the name of the iron-jawed men
I will stand up and say yes till the finish is come and gone.
God of all broken hearts, empty hands, sleeping soldiers,
God of all star-flung beaches of night sky,
I and my love-child stand up together to-day and sing: "Thanks,
    O God."

Baby Face

White Moon comes in on a baby face.
The shafts across her bed are flimmering.

Out on the land White Moon shines,
Shines and glimmers against gnarled shadows,
All silver to slow twisted shadows
Falling across the long road that runs from the house.

Keep a little of your beauty
And some of your flimmering silver
For her by the window to-night
Where you come in, White Moon.

The Year

I

A storm of white petals,
Buds throwing open baby fists
Into hands of broad flowers.

II

Red roses running upward,
Clambering to the clutches of life
Soaked in crimson.

III

Rabbles of tattered leaves
Holding golden flimsy hopes
Against the tramplings
Into the pits and gullies.

IV

Hoarfrost and silence:
Only the muffling
Of winds dark and lonesome—
Great lullabies to the long sleepers.

Drumnotes

Days of the dead men, Danny.
Drum for the dead, drum on your
    remembering heart.

Jaurès, a great love-heart of France,
    a slug of lead in the red valves.
Kitchener of Khartoum, tall, cold, proud,
    a shark's mouthful.
Franz Josef, the old man of forty haunted
    kingdoms, in a tomb with the Hapsburg
    fathers, moths eating a green uniform
    to tatters, worms taking all and leaving
    only bones and gold buttons, bones and
    iron crosses.
Jack London, Jim Riley, Verhaeren, riders to
    the republic of dreams.

Days of the dead, Danny.
Drum on your remembering heart.

Moonset

Leaves of poplars pick Japanese prints against the west.
Moon sand on the canal doubles the changing pictures.
      The moon's good-by ends pictures.
The west is empty. All else is empty. No moon-talk at all now.
      Only dark listening to dark.

Garden Wireless

How many feet ran with sunlight, water, and air?

What little devils shaken of laughter, cramming their little ribs
    with chuckles,

Fixed this lone red tulip, a woman's mouth of passion kisses, a
    nun's mouth of sweet thinking, here topping a straight line
    of green, a pillar stem?

Who hurled this bomb of red caresses?—nodding balloon-film
    shooting its wireless every fraction of a second these June
    days:
        Love me before I die;
        Love me—love me now.

Handfuls

    Blossoms of babies
Blinking their stories
Come soft
On the dusk and the babble;
Little red gamblers,
Handfuls that slept in the dust.

    Summers of rain,
Winters of drift,
Tell off the years;
And they go back

Who came soft—
Back to the sod,
To silence and dust;
Gray gamblers,
  Handfuls again.

Cool Tombs

When Abraham Lincoln was shoveled into the tombs, he forgot
the copperheads and the assassin . . . in the dust, in the cool
tombs.

And Ulysses Grant lost all thought of con men and Wall Street,
cash and collateral turned ashes . . . in the dust, in the cool
tombs.

Pocahontas' body, lovely as a poplar, sweet as a red haw in
November or a pawpaw in May, did she wonder? does she re-
member? . . . in the dust, in the cool tombs?

Take any streetful of people buying clothes and groceries, cheer-
ing a hero or throwing confetti and blowing tin horns . . . tell
me if the lovers are losers . . . tell me if any get more than
the lovers . . . in the dust . . . in the cool tombs.

SHENANDOAH

Shenandoah

In the Shenandoah Valley, one rider gray and one rider blue, and the sun on the riders wondering.

Piled in the Shenandoah, riders blue and riders gray, piled with shovels, one and another, dust in the Shenandoah taking them quicker than mothers take children done with play.

The blue nobody remembers, the gray nobody remembers, it's all old and old nowadays in the Shenandoah.

And all is young, a butter of dandelions slung on the turf, climbing blue flowers of the wishing woodlands wondering: a midnight purple violet claims the sun among old heads, among old dreams of repeating heads of a rider blue and a rider gray in the Shenandoah.

New Feet

Empty battlefields keep their phantoms.
Grass crawls over old gun wheels
And a nodding Canada thistle flings a purple
Into the summer's southwest wind,
Wrapping a root in the rust of a bayonet,
Reaching a blossom in rust of shrapnel.

Old Osawatomie

John Brown's body under the morning stars.
Six feet of dust under the morning stars.
And a panorama of war performs itself
Over the six-foot stage of circling armies.
Room for Gettysburg, Wilderness, Chickamauga,
On a six-foot stage of dust.

Grass

Pile the bodies high at Austerlitz and Waterloo.
Shovel them under and let me work—
       I am the grass; I cover all.

And pile them high at Gettysburg
And pile them high at Ypres and Verdun.
Shovel them under and let me work.
Two years, ten years, and passengers ask the conductor:
       What place is this?
       Where are we now?

       I am the grass.
       Let me work.

Flanders

Flanders, the name of a place, a country of people,
Spells itself with letters, is written in books.

"Where is Flanders?" was asked one time,
Flanders known only to those who lived there
And milked cows and made cheese and spoke the home lan-
    guage.

"Where is Flanders?" was asked.
And the slang adepts shot the reply: Search me.

A few thousand people milking cows, raising radishes,

On a land of salt grass and dunes, sand-swept with a sea-breath
     on it:
This was Flanders, the unknown, the quiet,
The place where cows hunted lush cuds of green on lowlands,
And the raw-boned plowmen took horses with long shanks
Out in the dawn to the sea-breath.

Flanders sat slow-spoken amid slow-swung windmills,
Slow-circling windmill arms turning north or west,
Turning to talk to the swaggering winds, the childish winds,
So Flanders sat with the heart of a kitchen girl
Washing wooden bowls in the winter sun by a window.

Gargoyle

I saw a mouth jeering. A smile of melted red iron ran over it. Its
     laugh was full of nails rattling. It was a child's dream of a
     mouth.
A fist hit the mouth: knuckles of gun-metal driven by an electric
     wrist and shoulder. It was a child's dream of an arm.
The fist hit the mouth over and over, again and again. The
     mouth bled melted iron, and laughed its laughter of nails
     rattling.
And I saw the more the fist pounded the more the mouth
     laughed. The fist is pounding and pounding, and the mouth
     answering.

Old Timers

I am an ancient reluctant conscript.

On the soup wagons of Xerxes I was a cleaner of pans.

On the march of Miltiades' phalanx I had a haft and head;
I had a bristling gleaming spear-handle.

Red-headed Cæsar picked me for a teamster.
He said, "Go to work, you Tuscan bastard,
Rome calls for a man who can drive horses."

The units of conquest led by Charles the Twelfth,
The whirling whimsical Napoleonic columns:
They saw me one of the horseshoers.

I trimmed the feet of a white horse Bonaparte swept the night
    stars with.

Lincoln said, "Get into the game; your nation takes you."
And I drove a wagon and team and I had my arm shot off
At Spottsylvania Court House.

I am an ancient reluctant conscript.

House

Two Swede families live downstairs and an Irish policeman up-
    stairs, and an old soldier, Uncle Joe.
Two Swede boys go upstairs and see Joe. His wife is dead, his only
    son is dead, and his two daughters in Missouri and Texas
    don't want him around.
The boys and Uncle Joe crack walnuts with a hammer on the bot-
    tom of a flatiron while the January wind howls and the zero
    air weaves laces on the window glass.
Joe tells the Swede boys all about Chickamauga and
    Chattanooga, how the Union soldiers crept in rain some-
    where a dark night and ran forward and killed many Rebels,
    took flags, held a hill, and won a victory told about in the his-
    tories in school.
Joe takes a piece of carpenter's chalk, draws lines on the floor and
    piles stove wood to show where six regiments were slaugh-
    tered climbing a slope.
"Here they went" and "Here they went," says Joe, and the January
    wind howls and the zero air weaves laces on the window
    glass.
The two Swede boys go downstairs with a big blur of guns, men,
    and hills in their heads. They eat herring and potatoes and
    tell the family war is a wonder and soldiers are a wonder.
One breaks out with a cry at supper: I wish we had a war now and
    I could be a soldier.

John Ericsson Day Memorial, 1918

Into the gulf and the pit of the dark night, the cold night, there is a man goes into the dark and the cold and when he comes back to his people he brings fire in his hands and they remember him in the years afterward as the fire bringer—they remember or forget—the man whose head kept singing to the want of his home, the want of his people.

For this man there is no name thought of—he has broken from jungles and the old oxen and the old wagons—circled the earth with ships—belted the earth with steel—swung with wings and a drumming motor in the high blue sky—shot his words on a wireless way through shattering sea storms:—out from the night and out from the jungles his head keeps singing—there is no road for him but on and on.

Against the sea bastions and the land bastions, against the great air pockets of stars and atoms, he points a finger, finds a release clutch, touches a button no man knew before.

The soldier with a smoking gun and a gas mask—the workshop man under the smokestacks and the blueprints—these two are brothers of the handshake never forgotten—for these two we give the salt tears of our eyes, the salute of red roses, the flame-won scarlet of poppies.

For the soldier who gives all, for the workshop man who gives all, for these the red bar is on the flag—the red bar is the heart's-blood of the mother who gave him, the land that gave him.

The gray foam and the great wheels of war go by and take all—and the years give mist and ashes—and our feet stand at these, the memory places of the known and the unknown, and our hands give a flame-won poppy—our hands touch the red bar of a flag for the sake of those who gave—and gave all.

Remembered Women

For a woman's face remembered as a spot of quick light on the
flat land of dark night,

For this memory of one mouth and a forehead they go on in the
gray rain and the mud, they go on among the boots and
guns.

The horizon ahead is a thousand fang flashes, it is a row of teeth
that bite on the flanks of night, the horizon sings of a new
kill and a big kill.

The horizon behind is a wall of dark etched with a memory, fixed
with a woman's face—they fight on and on, boots in the
mud and heads in the gray rain—for the women they hate
and the women they love—for the women they left behind,
they fight on.

Out of White Lips

Out of white lips a question: Shall seven million dead ask for their
blood a little land for the living wives and children, a little
land for the living brothers and sisters?

Out of white lips:—Shall they have only air that sweeps round the
earth for breath of their nostrils and no footing on the dirt of
the earth for their battle-drabbed, battle-soaked shoes?

Out of white lips:—Is the red in the flag the blood of a free man
on a piece of land his own or is it the red of a sheep slit in
the throat for mutton?

Out of white lips a white pain murmurs: Who shall have land?
Him who has stood ankle deep in the blood of his comrades,
in the red trenches dug in the land?

Memoir

Papa Joffre, the shoulders of him wide as the land of France.

We look on the shoulders filling the stage of the Chicago
Auditorium.

A fat mayor has spoken much English and the mud of his speech is crossed with quicksilver hisses elusive and rapid from floor and gallery.

A neat governor speaks English and the listeners ring chimes to his clear thoughts.

Joffre speaks a few words in French; this is a voice of the long firing line that runs from the salt sea dunes of Flanders to the white spear crags of the Swiss mountains.

This is the man on whose yes and no has hung the death of battalions and brigades; this man speaks of the tricolor of his country now melted in a great resolve with the starred bunting of Lincoln and Washington.

This is the hero of the Marne, massive, irreckonable; he lets tears roll down his cheek; they trickle a wet salt off his chin onto the blue coat.

There is a play of American hands and voices equal to seabreakers and a lift of white sun on a stony beach.

A Million Young Workmen, 1915

A million young workmen straight and strong lay stiff on the grass and roads,
And the million are now under soil and their rotting flesh will in the years feed roots of blood-red roses.
Yes, this million of young workmen slaughtered one another and never saw their red hands.
And oh, it would have been a great job of killing and a new and beautiful thing under the sun if the million knew why they hacked and tore each other to death.
The kings are grinning, the kaiser and the czar—they are alive riding in leather-seated motor cars, and they have their women and roses for ease, and they eat fresh-poached eggs for breakfast, new butter on toast, sitting in tall water-tight houses reading the news of war.
I dreamed a million ghosts of the young workmen rose in their shirts all soaked in crimson . . . and yelled:
God damn the grinning kings, God damn the kaiser and the czar.
                                                              Chicago, 1915.

Smoke

I sit in a chair and read the newspapers.

Millions of men go to war, acres of them are buried, guns and
ships broken, cities burned, villages sent up in smoke, and
children where cows are killed off amid hoarse barbecues
vanish like finger-rings of smoke in a north wind.

I sit in a chair and read the newspapers.

A Tall Man

The mouth of this man is a gaunt strong mouth.
The head of this man is a gaunt strong head.

The jaws of this man are bone of the Rocky Mountains, the
Appalachians.
The eyes of this man are chlorine of two sobbing oceans,
Foam, salt, green, wind, the changing unknown.
The neck of this man is pith of buffalo prairie, old longing and
new beckoning of corn belt or cotton belt,
Either a proud Sequoia trunk of the wilderness
Or huddling lumber of a sawmill waiting to be a roof.

Brother mystery to man and mob mystery,
Brother cryptic to lifted cryptic hands,
He is night and abyss, he is white sky of sun, he is the head of the
people.
The heart of him the red drops of the people,
The wish of him the steady gray-eagle crag-hunting flights of the
people.

Humble dust of a wheel-worn road,
Slashed sod under the iron-shining plow,
These of service in him, these and many cities, many borders,
many wrangles between Alaska and the Isthmus, between
the Isthmus and the Horn, and east and west of Omaha, and
east and west of Paris, Berlin, Petrograd.
The blood in his right wrist and the blood in his left wrist run
with the right wrist wisdom of the many and the left wrist
wisdom of the many.
It is the many he knows, the gaunt strong hunger of the many.

The Four Brothers

Notes for War Songs (November, 1917)

Make war songs out of these;
Make chants that repeat and weave.
Make rhythms up to the ragtime chatter of the machine guns;
Make slow-booming psalms up to the boom of the big guns.
Make a marching song of swinging arms and swinging legs,
  Going along,
  Going along,
On the roads from San Antonio to Athens, from Seattle to
  Bagdad —
The boys and men in winding lines of khaki, the circling squares
  of bayonet points.

Cowpunchers, cornhuskers, shopmen, ready in khaki;
Ballplayers, lumberjacks, ironworkers, ready in khaki;
A million, ten million, singing, "I am ready."
This the sun looks on between two seaboards,
In the land of Lincoln, in the land of Grant and Lee.

I heard one say, "I am ready to be killed."
I heard another say, "I am ready to be killed."
O sunburned clear-eyed boys!
I stand on sidewalks and you go by with drums and guns and
  bugles,
   You — and the flag!
And my heart tightens, a fist of something feels my throat
   When you go by,
You on the kaiser hunt, you and your faces saying, "I am ready to
  be killed."

They are hunting death,
Death for the one-armed mastoid kaiser.
They are after a Hohenzollern head:
There is no man-hunt of men remembered like this.

The four big brothers are out to kill.
France, Russia, Britain, America —
The four republics are sworn brothers to kill the kaiser.

Yes, this is the great man-hunt;
And the sun has never seen till now
Such a line of toothed and tusked man-killers,

In the blue of the upper sky,
In the green of the undersea,
In the red of winter dawns.
Eating to kill,
Sleeping to kill,
Asked by their mothers to kill,
Wished by four-fifths of the world to kill—
To cut the kaiser's throat,
To hack the kaiser's head,
To hang the kaiser on a high-horizon gibbet.

And is it nothing else than this?
Three times ten million men thirsting the blood
Of a half-cracked one-armed child of the German kings?
Three times ten million men asking the blood
Of a child born with his head wrong-shaped,
The blood of rotted kings in his veins?
If this were all, O God,
I would go to the far timbers
And look on the gray wolves
Tearing the throats of moose:
I would ask a wilder drunk of blood.

Look! It is four brothers in joined hands together.
            The people of bleeding France,
            The people of bleeding Russia,
            The people of Britain, the people of America—
These are the four brothers, these are the four republics.

At first I said it in anger as one who clenches his fist in wrath to
      fling his knuckles into the face of some one taunting;
Now I say it calmly as one who has thought it over and over again
      at night, among the mountains, by the sea-combers in storm.
I say now, by God, only fighters to-day will save the world, noth-
      ing but fighters will keep alive the names of those who left
      red prints of bleeding feet at Valley Forge in Christmas snow.
On the cross of Jesus, the sword of Napoleon, the skull of
      Shakespeare, the pen of Tom Jefferson, the ashes of
      Abraham Lincoln, or any sign of the red and running life
      poured out by the mothers of the world,
By the God of morning glories climbing blue the doors of quiet
      homes, by the God of tall hollyhocks laughing glad to

children in peaceful valleys, by the God of new mothers
wishing peace to sit at windows nursing babies,
I swear only reckless men, ready to throw away their lives by
hunger, deprivation, desperate clinging to a single purpose
imperturbable and undaunted, men with the primitive guts
of rebellion,
Only fighters gaunt with the red brand of labor's sorrow on their
brows and labor's terrible pride in their blood, men with
souls asking danger—only these will save and keep the four
big brothers.

Good-night is the word, good-night to the kings, to the czars,
        Good-night to the kaiser.
The breakdown and the fade-away begins.
The shadow of a great broom, ready to sweep out the trash, is here.

One finger is raised that counts the czar,
The ghost who beckoned men who come no more—
The czar gone to the winds on God's great dustpan,
The czar a pinch of nothing,
The last of the gibbering Romanoffs.

Out and good-night—
The ghosts of the summer palaces
And the ghosts of the winter palaces!
Out and out, good-night to the kings, the czars, the kaisers.

Another finger will speak,
And the kaiser, the ghost who gestures a hundred million
sleeping-waking ghosts,
The kaiser will go onto God's great dustpan—
The last of the gibbering Hohenzollerns.
Look! God pities this trash, God waits with a broom and a dust-
pan,
God knows a finger will speak and count them out.

It is written in the stars;
It is spoken on the walls;
It clicks in the fire-white zigzag of the Atlantic wireless;
It mutters in the bastions of thousand-mile continents;
It sings in a whistle on the midnight winds from Walla Walla to
Mesopotamia:
Out and good-night.

The millions slow in khaki,
The millions learning *Turkey in the Straw* and *John Brown's Body*,
The millions remembering windrows of dead at Gettysburg,
    Chickamauga, and Spottsylvania Court House,
The millions dreaming of the morning star of Appomattox,
The millions easy and calm with guns and steel, planes and prows:
        There is a hammering, drumming hell to come.
        The killing gangs are on the way.

God takes one year for a job.
God takes ten years or a million.
God knows when a doom is written.
God knows this job will be done and the words spoken:
Out and good-night.
        The red tubes will run,
        And the great price be paid,
        And the homes empty,
        And the wives wishing,
        And the mothers wishing.
There is only one way now, only the way of the red tubes and the
    great price.

        Well . . .
Maybe the morning sun is a five-cent yellow balloon,
And the evening stars the joke of a God gone crazy.
Maybe the mothers of the world,
And the life that pours from their torsal folds—
Maybe it's all a lie sworn by liars,
And a God with a cackling laughter says:
"I, the Almighty God,
I have made all this,
I have made it for kaisers, czars, and kings."

Three times ten million men say: No.
Three times ten million men say:
        God is a God of the People.
And the God who made the world
        And fixed the morning sun,
        And flung the evening stars,
        And shaped the baby hands of life,
This is the God of the Four Brothers;
This is the God of bleeding France and bleeding Russia;
This is the God of the people of Britain and America.

The graves from the Irish Sea to the Caucasus peaks are ten times
   a million.
The stubs and stumps of arms and legs, the eyesockets empty, the
   cripples, ten times a million.
The crimson thumb-print of this anathema is on the door panels
   of a hundred million homes.
Cows gone, mothers on sick-beds, children cry a hunger and no
   milk comes in the noon-time or at night.
The death-yells of it all, the torn throats of men in ditches calling
   for water, the shadows and the hacking lungs in dugouts, the
   steel paws that clutch and squeeze a scarlet drain day by
   day—the storm of it is hell.
But look! child! the storm is blowing for a clean air.

Look! the four brothers march
And hurl their big shoulders
And swear the job shall be done.

Out of the wild finger-writing north and south, east and west, over
   the blood-crossed, blood-dusty ball of earth,
Out of it all a God who knows is sweeping clean,
Out of it all a God who sees and pierces through, is breaking and
   cleaning out an old thousand years, is making ready for a
   new thousand years.
The four brothers shall be five and more.

Under the chimneys of the winter time the children of the world
   shall sing new songs.
Among the rocking restless cradles the mothers of the world shall
   sing new sleepy-time songs.

Alphabetical Index of Titles

Alphabetical Index of First Lines

DOVER·THRIFT·EDITIONS

POETRY

A SHROPSHIRE LAD, A. E. Housman. 64pp. 26468-8 $1.00

LYRIC POEMS, John Keats. 80pp. 26871-3 $1.00

GUNGA DIN AND OTHER FAVORITE POEMS, Rudyard Kipling. 80pp. 26471-8 $1.00

THE CONGO AND OTHER POEMS, Vachel Lindsay. 96pp. 27272-9 $1.50

EVANGELINE AND OTHER POEMS, Henry Wadsworth Longfellow. 64pp. 28255-4 $1.00

FAVORITE POEMS, Henry Wadsworth Longfellow. 96pp. 27273-7 $1.00

"TO HIS COY MISTRESS" AND OTHER POEMS, Andrew Marvell. 64pp. 29544-3 $1.00

SPOON RIVER ANTHOLOGY, Edgar Lee Masters. 144pp. 27275-3 $1.50

RENASCENCE AND OTHER POEMS, Edna St. Vincent Millay. 64pp. (Available in U.S. only.) 26873-X $1.00

SELECTED POEMS, John Milton. 128pp. 27554-X $1.50

CIVIL WAR POETRY: An Anthology, Paul Negri (ed.). 128pp. 29883-3 $1.50

ENGLISH VICTORIAN POETRY: AN ANTHOLOGY, Paul Negri (ed.). 256pp. 40425-0 $2.00

GREAT SONNETS, Paul Negri (ed.). 96pp. 28052-7 $1.00

THE RAVEN AND OTHER FAVORITE POEMS, Edgar Allan Poe. 64pp. 26685-0 $1.00

ESSAY ON MAN AND OTHER POEMS, Alexander Pope. 128pp. 28053-5 $1.50

EARLY POEMS, Ezra Pound. 80pp. (Available in U.S. only.) 28745-9 $1.00

GREAT POEMS BY AMERICAN WOMEN: An Anthology, Susan L. Rattiner (ed.). 224pp. (Available in U.S. only.) 40164-2 $2.00

LITTLE ORPHANT ANNIE AND OTHER POEMS, James Whitcomb Riley. 80pp. 28260-0 $1.00

"MINIVER CHEEVY" AND OTHER POEMS, Edwin Arlington Robinson. 64pp. 28756-4 $1.00

GOBLIN MARKET AND OTHER POEMS, Christina Rossetti. 64pp. 28055-1 $1.00

CHICAGO POEMS, Carl Sandburg. 80pp. 28057-8 $1.00

THE SHOOTING OF DAN MCGREW AND OTHER POEMS, Robert Service. 96pp. (Available in U.S. only.) 27556-6 $1.50

COMPLETE SONNETS, William Shakespeare. 80pp. 26686-9 $1.00

SELECTED POEMS, Percy Bysshe Shelley. 128pp. 27558-2 $1.50

AFRICAN-AMERICAN POETRY: An Anthology, 1773–1930, Joan R. Sherman (ed.). 96pp. 29604-0 $1.00

100 BEST-LOVED POEMS, Philip Smith (ed.). 96pp. 28553-7 $1.00

NATIVE AMERICAN SONGS AND POEMS: An Anthology, Brian Swann (ed.). 64pp. 29450-1 $1.00

SELECTED POEMS, Alfred Lord Tennyson. 112pp. 27282-6 $1.50

AENEID, Vergil (Publius Vergilius Maro). 256pp. 28749-1 $2.00

CHRISTMAS CAROLS: COMPLETE VERSES, Shane Weller (ed.). 64pp. 27397-0 $1.00

GREAT LOVE POEMS, Shane Weller (ed.). 128pp. 27284-2 $1.00

CIVIL WAR POETRY AND PROSE, Walt Whitman. 96pp. 28507-3 $1.00

SELECTED POEMS, Walt Whitman. 128pp. 26878-0 $1.00

THE BALLAD OF READING GAOL AND OTHER POEMS, Oscar Wilde. 64pp. 27072-6 $1.00

EARLY POEMS, William Carlos Williams. 64pp. (Available in U.S. only.) 29294-0 $1.00

FAVORITE POEMS, William Wordsworth. 80pp. 27073-4 $1.00

WORLD WAR ONE BRITISH POETS: Brooke, Owen, Sassoon, Rosenberg, and Others, Candace Ward (ed.). (Available in U.S. only.) 29568-0 $1.00

EARLY POEMS, William Butler Yeats. 128pp. 27808-5 $1.50

"EASTER, 1916" AND OTHER POEMS, William Butler Yeats. 80pp. (Available in U.S. only.) 29771-3 $1.00

DOVER·THRIFT·EDITIONS

FICTION

FLATLAND: A ROMANCE OF MANY DIMENSIONS, Edwin A. Abbott. 96pp. 27263-X $1.00

SHORT STORIES, Louisa May Alcott. 64pp. 29063-8 $1.00

WINESBURG, OHIO, Sherwood Anderson. 160pp. 28269-4 $2.00

PERSUASION, Jane Austen. 224pp. 29555-9 $2.00

PRIDE AND PREJUDICE, Jane Austen. 272pp. 28473-5 $2.00

SENSE AND SENSIBILITY, Jane Austen. 272pp. 29049-2 $2.00

LOOKING BACKWARD, Edward Bellamy. 160pp. 29038-7 $2.00

BEOWULF, Beowulf (trans. by R. K. Gordon). 64pp. 27264-8 $1.00

CIVIL WAR STORIES, Ambrose Bierce. 128pp. 28038-1 $1.00

"THE MOONLIT ROAD" AND OTHER GHOST AND HORROR STORIES, Ambrose Bierce (John Grafton, ed.) 96pp. 40056-5 $1.00

WUTHERING HEIGHTS, Emily Brontë. 256pp. 29256-8 $2.00

THE THIRTY-NINE STEPS, John Buchan. 96pp. 28201-5 $1.50

TARZAN OF THE APES, Edgar Rice Burroughs. 224pp. (Available in U.S. only.) 29570-2 $2.00

ALICE'S ADVENTURES IN WONDERLAND, Lewis Carroll. 96pp. 27543-4 $1.00

THROUGH THE LOOKING-GLASS, Lewis Carroll. 128pp. 40878-7 $1.50

MY ÁNTONIA, Willa Cather. 176pp. 28240-6 $2.00

O PIONEERS!, Willa Cather. 128pp. 27785-2 $1.00

PAUL'S CASE AND OTHER STORIES, Willa Cather. 64pp. 29057-3 $1.00

FIVE GREAT SHORT STORIES, Anton Chekhov. 96pp. 26463-7 $1.00

TALES OF CONJURE AND THE COLOR LINE, Charles Waddell Chesnutt. 128pp. 40426-9 $1.50

FAVORITE FATHER BROWN STORIES, G. K. Chesterton. 96pp. 27545-0 $1.00

THE AWAKENING, Kate Chopin. 128pp. 27786-0 $1.00

A PAIR OF SILK STOCKINGS AND OTHER STORIES, Kate Chopin. 64pp. 29264-9 $1.00

HEART OF DARKNESS, Joseph Conrad. 80pp. 26464-5 $1.00

LORD JIM, Joseph Conrad. 256pp. 40650-4 $2.00

THE SECRET SHARER AND OTHER STORIES, Joseph Conrad. 128pp. 27546-9 $1.00

THE "LITTLE REGIMENT" AND OTHER CIVIL WAR STORIES, Stephen Crane. 80pp. 29557-5 $1.00

THE OPEN BOAT AND OTHER STORIES, Stephen Crane. 128pp. 27547-7 $1.50

THE RED BADGE OF COURAGE, Stephen Crane. 112pp. 26465-3 $1.00

MOLL FLANDERS, Daniel Defoe. 256pp. 29093-X $2.00

ROBINSON CRUSOE, Daniel Defoe. 288pp. 40427-7 $2.00

A CHRISTMAS CAROL, Charles Dickens. 80pp. 26865-9 $1.00

THE CRICKET ON THE HEARTH AND OTHER CHRISTMAS STORIES, Charles Dickens. 128pp. 28039-X $1.00

A TALE OF TWO CITIES, Charles Dickens. 304pp. 40651-2 $2.00

THE DOUBLE, Fyodor Dostoyevsky. 128pp. 29572-9 $1.50

THE GAMBLER, Fyodor Dostoyevsky. 112pp. 29081-6 $1.50

NOTES FROM THE UNDERGROUND, Fyodor Dostoyevsky. 96pp. 27053-X $1.00

THE ADVENTURE OF THE DANCING MEN AND OTHER STORIES, Sir Arthur Conan Doyle. 80pp. 29558-3 $1.00

THE HOUND OF THE BASKERVILLES, Arthur Conan Doyle. 128pp. 28214-7 $1.50

THE LOST WORLD, Arthur Conan Doyle. 176pp. 40060-3 $1.50

DOVER · THRIFT · EDITIONS

FICTION

SIX GREAT SHERLOCK HOLMES STORIES, Sir Arthur Conan Doyle. 112pp. 27055-6 $1.00

SILAS MARNER, George Eliot. 160pp. 29246-0 $1.50

THIS SIDE OF PARADISE, F. Scott Fitzgerald. 208pp. 28999-0 $2.00

"THE DIAMOND AS BIG AS THE RITZ" AND OTHER STORIES, F. Scott Fitzgerald. 29991-0 $2.00

THE REVOLT OF "MOTHER" AND OTHER STORIES, Mary E. Wilkins Freeman. 128pp. 40428-5 $1.50

MADAME BOVARY, Gustave Flaubert. 256pp. 29257-6 $2.00

WHERE ANGELS FEAR TO TREAD, E. M. Forster. 128pp. (Available in U.S. only.) 27791-7 $1.50

A ROOM WITH A VIEW, E. M. Forster. 176pp. (Available in U.S. only.) 28467-0 $2.00

THE IMMORALIST, André Gide. 112pp. (Available in U.S. only.) 29237-1 $1.50

"THE YELLOW WALLPAPER" AND OTHER STORIES, Charlotte Perkins Gilman. 80pp. 29857-4 $1.00

HERLAND, Charlotte Perkins Gilman. 128pp. 40429-3 $1.50

THE OVERCOAT AND OTHER STORIES, Nikolai Gogol. 112pp. 27057-2 $1.50

GREAT GHOST STORIES, John Grafton (ed.). 112pp. 27270-2 $1.00

DETECTION BY GASLIGHT, Douglas G. Greene (ed.). 272pp. 29928-7 $2.00

THE MABINOGION, Lady Charlotte E. Guest. 192pp. 29541-9 $2.00

"THE FIDDLER OF THE REELS" AND OTHER SHORT STORIES, Thomas Hardy. 80pp. 29960-0 $1.50

THE LUCK OF ROARING CAMP AND OTHER STORIES, Bret Harte. 96pp. 27271-0 $1.00

THE SCARLET LETTER, Nathaniel Hawthorne. 192pp. 28048-9 $2.00

YOUNG GOODMAN BROWN AND OTHER STORIES, Nathaniel Hawthorne. 128pp. 27060-2 $1.00

THE GIFT OF THE MAGI AND OTHER SHORT STORIES, O. Henry. 96pp. 27061-0 $1.00

THE NUTCRACKER AND THE GOLDEN POT, E. T. A. Hoffmann. 128pp. 27806-9 $1.00

THE BEAST IN THE JUNGLE AND OTHER STORIES, Henry James. 128pp. 27552-3 $1.50

DAISY MILLER, Henry James. 64pp. 28773-4 $1.00

THE TURN OF THE SCREW, Henry James. 96pp. 26684-2 $1.00

WASHINGTON SQUARE, Henry James. 176pp. 40431-5 $2.00

THE COUNTRY OF THE POINTED FIRS, Sarah Orne Jewett. 96pp. 28196-5 $1.00

THE AUTOBIOGRAPHY OF AN EX-COLORED MAN, James Weldon Johnson. 112pp. 28512-X $1.00

DUBLINERS, James Joyce. 160pp. 26870-5 $1.00

A PORTRAIT OF THE ARTIST AS A YOUNG MAN, James Joyce. 192pp. 28050-0 $2.00

THE METAMORPHOSIS AND OTHER STORIES, Franz Kafka. 96pp. 29030-1 $1.50

THE MAN WHO WOULD BE KING AND OTHER STORIES, Rudyard Kipling. 128pp. 28051-9 $1.50

YOU KNOW ME AL, Ring Lardner. 128pp. 28513-8 $1.50

SELECTED SHORT STORIES, D. H. Lawrence. 128pp. 27794-1 $1.50

GREEN TEA AND OTHER GHOST STORIES, J. Sheridan LeFanu. 96pp. 27795-X $1.50

SHORT STORIES, Theodore Dreiser. 112pp. 28215-5 $1.50

THE CALL OF THE WILD, Jack London. 64pp. 26472-6 $1.00

FIVE GREAT SHORT STORIES, Jack London. 96pp. 27063-7 $1.00

WHITE FANG, Jack London. 160pp. 26968-X $1.00

DEATH IN VENICE, Thomas Mann. 96pp. (Available in U.S. only.) 28714-9 $1.00

IN A GERMAN PENSION: 13 Stories, Katherine Mansfield. 112pp. 28719-X $1.50

THE MOON AND SIXPENCE, W. Somerset Maugham. 176pp. (Available in U.S. only.) 28731-9 $2.00

DOVER · THRIFT · EDITIONS

FICTION

THE NECKLACE AND OTHER SHORT STORIES, Guy de Maupassant. 128pp. 27064-5 $1.00
BARTLEBY AND BENITO CERENO, Herman Melville. 112pp. 26473-4 $1.00
THE OIL JAR AND OTHER STORIES, Luigi Pirandello. 96pp. 28459-X $1.00
THE GOLD-BUG AND OTHER TALES, Edgar Allan Poe. 128pp. 26875-6 $1.00
TALES OF TERROR AND DETECTION, Edgar Allan Poe. 96pp. 28744-0 $1.00
THE QUEEN OF SPADES AND OTHER STORIES, Alexander Pushkin. 128pp. 28054-3 $1.50
SREDNI VASHTAR AND OTHER STORIES, Saki (H. H. Munro). 96pp. 28521-9 $1.00
THE STORY OF AN AFRICAN FARM, Olive Schreiner. 256pp. 40165-0 $2.00
FRANKENSTEIN, Mary Shelley. 176pp. 28211-2 $1.00
THREE LIVES, Gertrude Stein. 176pp. (Available in U.S. only.) 28059-4 $2.00
THE STRANGE CASE OF DR. JEKYLL AND MR. HYDE, Robert Louis Stevenson. 64pp. 26688-5 $1.00
TREASURE ISLAND, Robert Louis Stevenson. 160pp. 27559-0 $1.50
GULLIVER'S TRAVELS, Jonathan Swift. 240pp. 29273-8 $2.00
THE KREUTZER SONATA AND OTHER SHORT STORIES, Leo Tolstoy. 144pp. 27805-0 $1.50
THE WARDEN, Anthony Trollope. 176pp. 40076-X $2.00
FIRST LOVE AND DIARY OF A SUPERFLUOUS MAN, Ivan Turgenev. 96pp. 28775-0 $1.50
FATHERS AND SONS, Ivan Turgenev. 176pp. 40073-5 $2.00
ADVENTURES OF HUCKLEBERRY FINN, Mark Twain. 224pp. 28061-6 $2.00
THE ADVENTURES OF TOM SAWYER, Mark Twain. 192pp. 40077-8 $2.00
THE MYSTERIOUS STRANGER AND OTHER STORIES, Mark Twain. 128pp. 27069-6 $1.00
HUMOROUS STORIES AND SKETCHES, Mark Twain. 80pp. 29279-7 $1.00
CANDIDE, Voltaire (François-Marie Arouet). 112pp. 26689-3 $1.00
GREAT SHORT STORIES BY AMERICAN WOMEN, Candace Ward (ed.). 192pp. 28776-9 $2.00
"THE COUNTRY OF THE BLIND" AND OTHER SCIENCE-FICTION STORIES, H. G. Wells. 160pp. (Available in U.S. only.) 29569-9 $1.00
THE ISLAND OF DR. MOREAU, H. G. Wells. 112pp. (Available in U.S. only.) 29027-1 $1.50
THE INVISIBLE MAN, H. G. Wells. 112pp. (Available in U.S. only.) 27071-8 $1.00
THE TIME MACHINE, H. G. Wells. 80pp. (Available in U.S. only.) 28472-7 $1.00
THE WAR OF THE WORLDS, H. G. Wells. 160pp. (Available in U.S. only.) 29506-0 $1.00
ETHAN FROME, Edith Wharton. 96pp. 26690-7 $1.00
SHORT STORIES, Edith Wharton. 128pp. 28235-X $1.50
THE AGE OF INNOCENCE, Edith Wharton. 288pp. 29803-5 $2.00
THE PICTURE OF DORIAN GRAY, Oscar Wilde. 192pp. 27807-7 $1.50
JACOB'S ROOM, Virginia Woolf. 144pp. (Available in U.S. only.) 40109-X $1.50
MONDAY OR TUESDAY: Eight Stories, Virginia Woolf. 64pp. (Available in U.S. only.) 29453-6 $1.00

NONFICTION

POETICS, Aristotle. 64pp. 29577-X $1.00
NICOMACHEAN ETHICS, Aristotle. 256pp. 40096-4 $2.00
MEDITATIONS, Marcus Aurelius. 128pp. 29823-X $1.50
THE LAND OF LITTLE RAIN, Mary Austin. 96pp. 29037-9 $1.50
THE DEVIL'S DICTIONARY, Ambrose Bierce. 144pp. 27542-6 $1.00
THE ANALECTS, Confucius. 128pp. 28484-0 $2.00
CONFESSIONS OF AN ENGLISH OPIUM EATER, Thomas De Quincey. 80pp. 28742-4 $1.00
NARRATIVE OF THE LIFE OF FREDERICK DOUGLASS, Frederick Douglass. 96pp. 28499-9 $1.00